WIND, WATER & TIME
Canyons of the Southwest

LARRY ROGERS

Acknowledgements

Thank you to Eric and Norma Curby for many miles traveled and hours spent in search of wild places. Your companionship makes my work fun.

Thank you to my son, Bryan, for your inspiration and design guidance.

Print Books by Larry Rogers

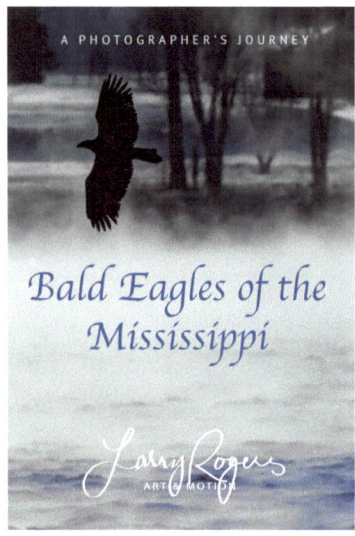

Bald Eagles of the Mississippi

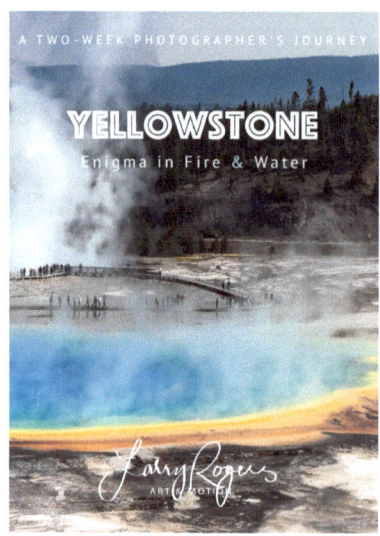

Yellowstone: Enignma in Fire & Water

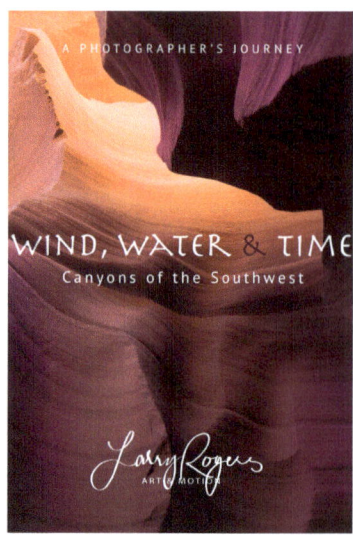

Wind, Water & Time

eBooks by Larry Rogers

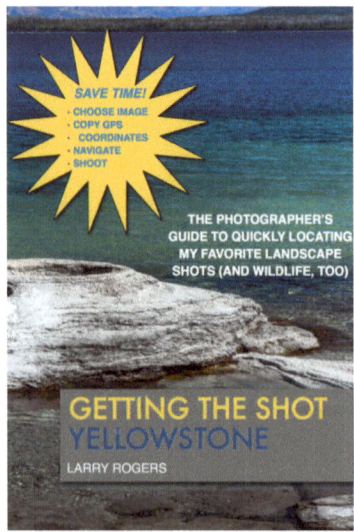

Getting the Shot: Yellowstone

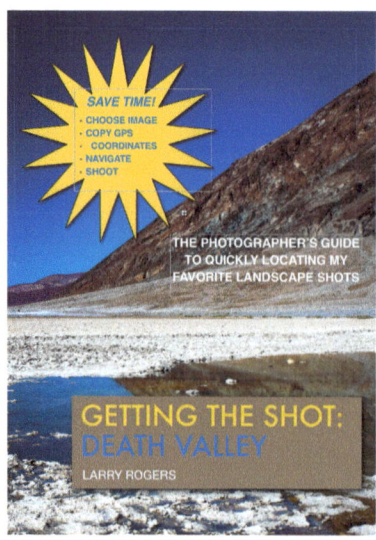

Getting the Shot: Death Valley

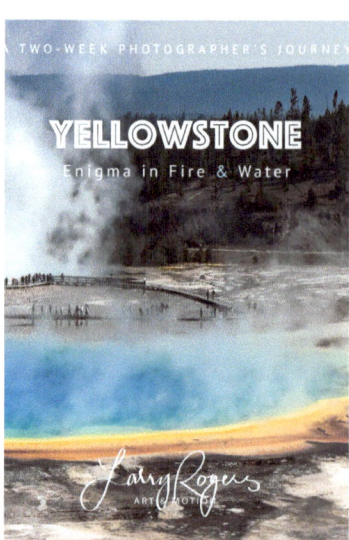

Yellowstone: Enignma in Fire & Water

Copyright Larry Rogers 2019, All rights reserved.
Print ISBN 9781794328914

"I was standing on the highest mountain of them all, and round about beneath me was the whole hoop of the world.

And while I stood there I saw more than I can tell and I understood more than I saw; for I was seeing in a sacred manner the shapes of all things in the spirit, and the shape of all shapes as they must live together like one being."

Black Elk

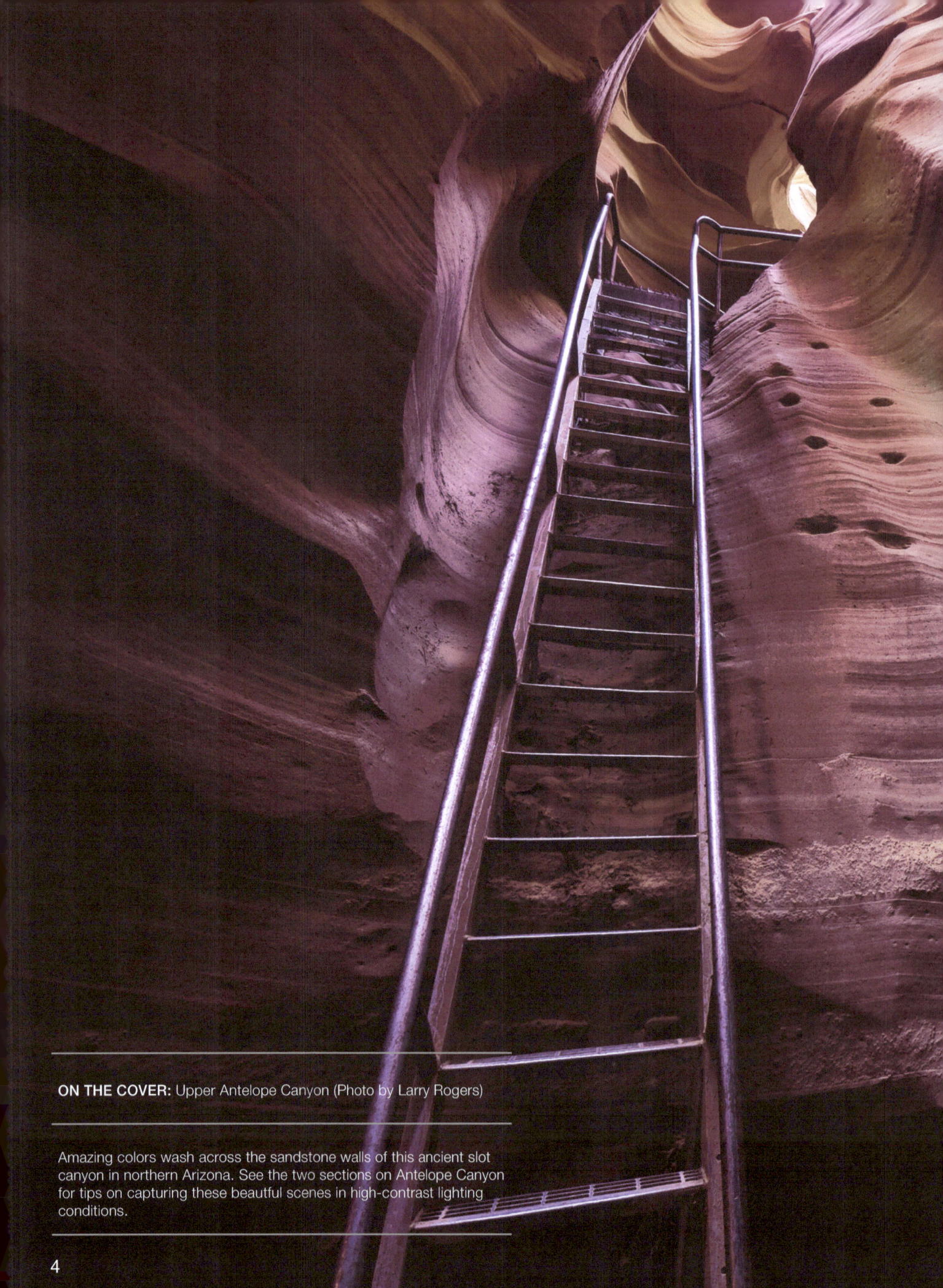

ON THE COVER: Upper Antelope Canyon (Photo by Larry Rogers)

Amazing colors wash across the sandstone walls of this ancient slot canyon in northern Arizona. See the two sections on Antelope Canyon for tips on capturing these beautiful scenes in high-contrast lighting conditions.

INSIDE >

06	Introduction to the Canyons of the Southwest
14	Valley of Fire State Park, Nevada
17	Zion National Park, Utah
25	Bryce Canyon National Park, Utah
30	Grand Staircase-Escalante National Monument, Utah
34	Lower Antelope Canyon Navajo Tribal Park, Arizona
38	Upper Antelope Canyon Navajo Tribal Park, Arizona
40	Monument Valley Navajo Tribal Park, Arizona
42	The Goosenecks State Park, Utah
44	Capitol Reef National Park, Utah
46	Canyonlands National Park, Utah
50	Arches National Park, Utah
52	Dead Horse Point State Park, Utah
54	Goblin Valley State Park, Utah
56	Sego Canyon, Utah
58	Beyond the Click
60	About the Author

Lower Antelope Canyon (Photo by Larry Rogers)

Walk with ancients. Centuries-old hand and foot impressions parallel a modern ladder. Today, this stairway is the path to enter or exit the deep (north) end of the canyon. At the opposite end, entry into the canyon is at ground level. From that point, the canyon floor falls approximately 120 feet over its length of 1,500 feet.

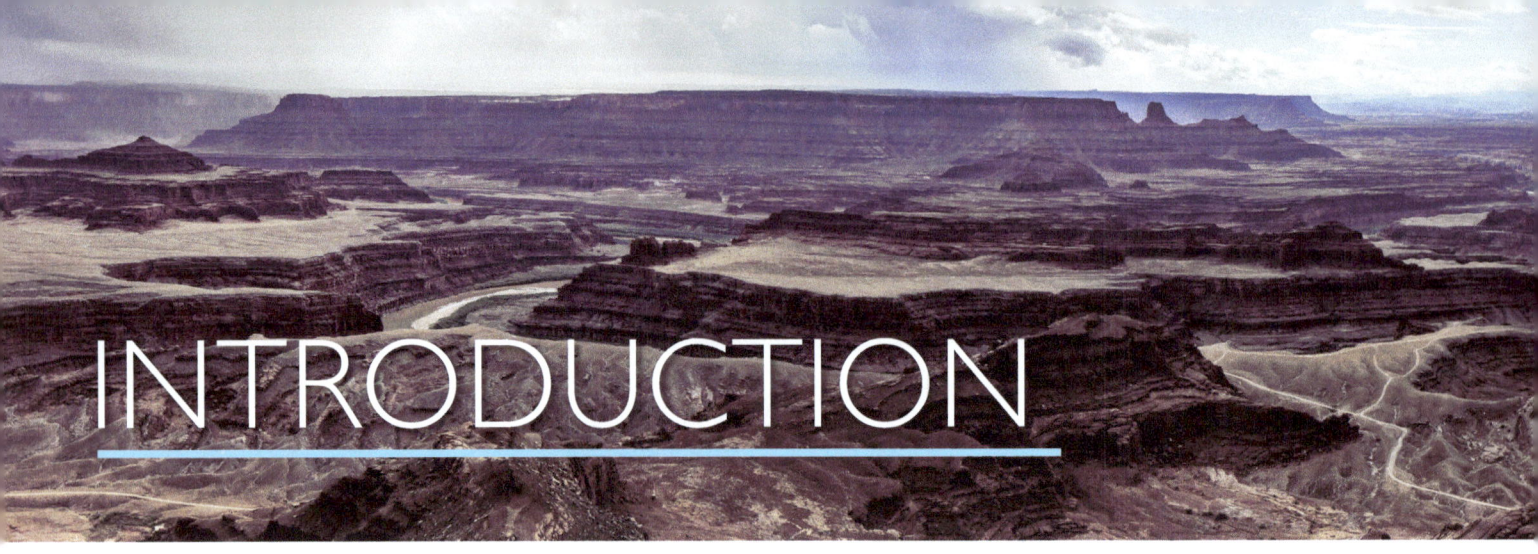

INTRODUCTION

The story of Wind, Water, & Time goes back our earliest understanding of Earth's geologic timeline. The science of geology is a discussion that should be led by people with much more education on that science than me. I wrote this book to share my art and my photographic journey through the southwest United States, a journey that began about twenty years ago and continues today. I will comment on the wonders of geology, but I'll leave detailed discussion of the science itself to the experts.

Once upon a time, I was a passenger on a commercial aircraft flying 30,000 feet above the Colorado River Plateau. Looking down after a time, I felt I was admiring artwork. "It's beautiful! What a shame," I thought, "there are no people in sight down there, no towns no one to enjoy this, and (I'm guessing) not one person on this plane has even noticed the art of it all." I remember thinking that I should one day go down there, with camera in hand, to capture and share its beauty.

I hope you enjoy the photo tour and the tips sprinkled in here and there. This is a brief introduction to the topics and the photo tour to come in the following pages.

The photo tour is laid out as a person might travel by car on a tour of the canyons of the southwest, from west to east, starting at the Las Vegas airport as I did on my first visit to the area several years ago, and that I have repeated a number of time since. Let's get started!

Valley of Fire State Park. I found what I believe to be signs of ancient man just about 50 miles northeast of Las Vegas McCarran Airport. Interesting rock formations abound here, but what I found unique about this place is evidence of ancient artists working in wet clay or sand that now sits preserved for us to study and enjoy. I will show you what I believe to be the imprint of a sandal worn by our ancient ancestor while he or she drew designs in wet sand with a stick or similar tool, and a few other things, too.

Zion National Park. During a visit to this historic national treasure, you can hike along the shores of the Virgin River which now flows between massive vertical walls that rise high above the canyon floor. Serious hikers may wish to pass through 'The Narrows,' or climb the high trail to Angel's Landing. Plan carefully, as you will not be able to drive to your trailhead, except in winter, because all of Zion must be accessed by bus.

Bryce Canyon National Park. Unlike most canyons of the southwest, your first glimpse of Bryce Canyon will be from high above the canyon floor. From the main road, you will be greeted with a view of bright sandstone pinnacles rising up from the

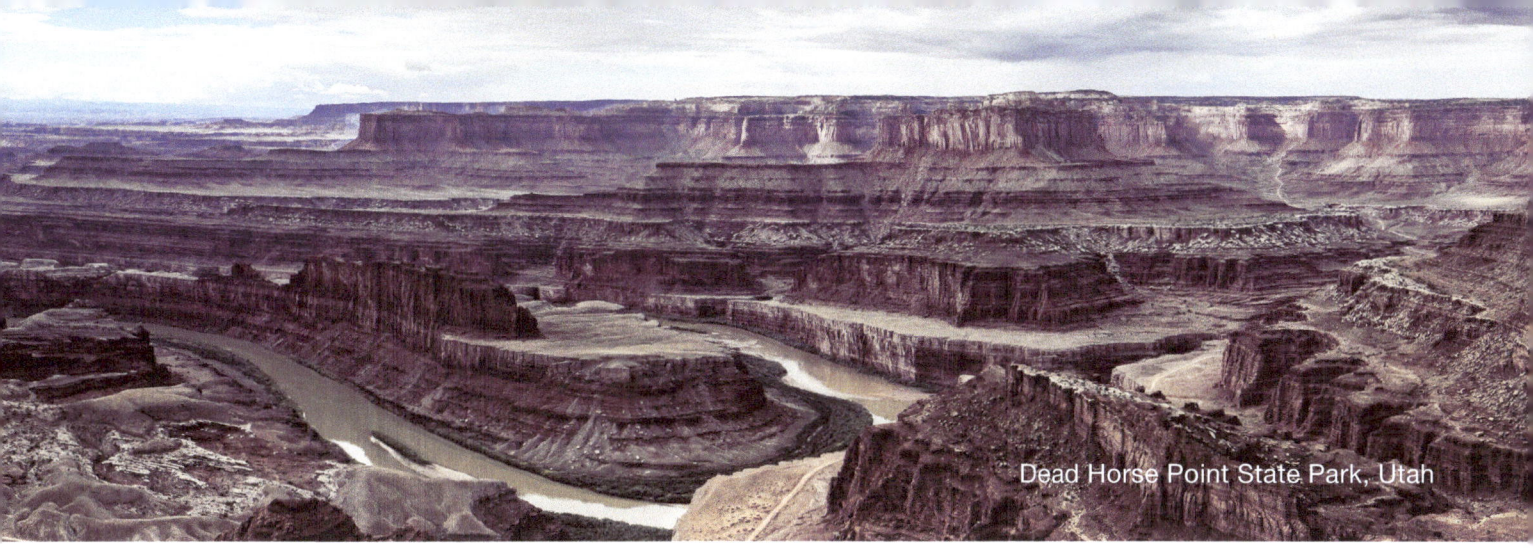

Dead Horse Point State Park, Utah

canyon floor in a splash of color and contrast. There are opportunities to hike down into the lower canyon for those so inclined. Pick up a national park map for more information on hiking trails. I will share a few photos of spectacular views from Bryce Canyon.

Grand Staircase-Escalante National Monument. This out-of-way gem has some of the most striking rock walls in the southwest. Scan vertical canyon walls with binoculars - you may find an adventurous climber (or two) up there!

There are also a number of 'wild' slot canyons, those not located in commercial areas nor having fulltime tour operators. I have included a few photos from one such slot canyon in later pages. Most of Grand Staircase is relatively easy to hike. Wild slot canyons, on the other hand, may be difficult to find and to hike through. More information can be found online.

Lower Antelope Canyon. On my short list of places that I simply cannot stop visiting over and over is this place and it's neighbor, the upper canyon. You will need a Navajo tour guide, which you can book at the tribe's official operators located on site, just south of Page, Arizona. Photographers should definitely pay the small extra charge for a 'photo tour.' The popularity of this place has risen to a point where tours are getting too crowded for good photography. Photo tours allow tripods, which are essential to capture the subtle tones you will see in my photos in the coming pages. A good tip for your guide will go a long way toward getting unobstructed shots. It is also a good idea to plan for multiple trips through the canyon. I see new things every time I visit .

Upper Antelope Canyon. With its own personality, different from that of its 'lower' neighbor, the upper canyon is known for its mid-day beams of light. Navajo guides will let you know the best times and locations. Photographer tours are usually scheduled during peak times for light beams. Like the lower canyon, a good tip goes a long way and allowing time for multiple trips may pay off in better photos.

Monument Valley Tribal Park. There are few places in North America that have been seen in more ads and movie classics than this classic of Americana. Hollywood producer John Ford so loved a point jutting out from a high mesa that the tribe named it for him. I love the fact that the tribe responsible for management has maintained the land as it was thousands of years ago. This is a must-see location in northern Arizona, just south of Mexican Hat, Utah.

Arches National Park. Located just outside the town of Moab in southeast Utah, Arches National Park may be one of the most convenient of all national parks to national parks to visit from a nearby town. It is certainly not short on photo attractions,

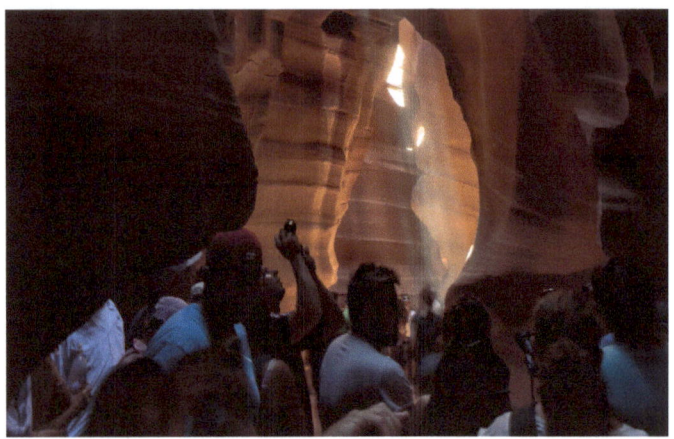

Things get tight in Upper Antelope Canyon. Even on a photographer tour, people crowd in to get a shot of the famous light beams.

the most famous of which is Delicate Arch which has made the cover of many travel publications. Be sure to walk some of the relatively easy trails to get up close and personal with awesome sandstone arch formations, like Double Arch in the Windows district. Those of you who enjoy astrophotography will find the night sky in Arches simply exquisite. Double Arch is a favorite for night sky photography..

Arches has several unique and different regions - Courthouse Towers, Petrified Dunes, Windows, Fiery Furnace and Devil's Garden. A number of reasonably moderate hikes are shown on park guides.

Canyonlands National Park. This massive area includes four districts - Island in the Sky, The Maze, Needles, and Horseshoe Canyon. It is impossible to do justice to Canyonlands in a few pages. Perhaps I will devote an entire book to it one day. For those desiring an unforgettable, up-close experience here, drive the White Rim Trail - or, a better idea, hire a guide with a sturdy four-wheel drive Jeep to drive you through. For a relatively easy walk to an unforgettable experience, take the short hike to Mesa Arch.

Goblin Valley State Park. This state park near Moab, Utah, is easily the strangest landscape I have seen in North America. Imagine gigantic sandstone mushrooms as far as the eye can see. I recommend getting out of the car and hiking through them, but don't lose sight of the visitor's shelter. Get lost, and you might be in amongst the mushrooms for a long time! I know, because it happend to me. Let me emphasize that you have to get out of the car and take the short walk down amongst the stone formations in order to get an appreciation for their size.

Sego Canyon. Yet another attraction in close vicinity to the town of Moab, Utah, is this site where some of the oldest pictographs in the southwest can be seen. Unlike petroglyphs that were carved into stone, pictographs were painted with natural pigments. Even with GPS coordinates, the site of these pictographs can be very hard to find. Be patient, look closely at the sandstone walls for very slight discolorations. Time and vandalism have taken a toll on them. Wait for the right light, good photos are still possible. Don't feel bad if you have trouble finding them, I drove right past them several times before stopping to ask a local road grader operator, who gave me precise instructions, "... then turn left at the twisted cedar tree..."

The Photo Tour (starting on page 14)

I have included many of my personal favorite photos from a number of visits to the canyons listed above. In the captions, I have also made suggestions on photographic techniques that I used to get these images. Whether you are reading this as a photographer or vactioner, I hope you enjoy the tour!

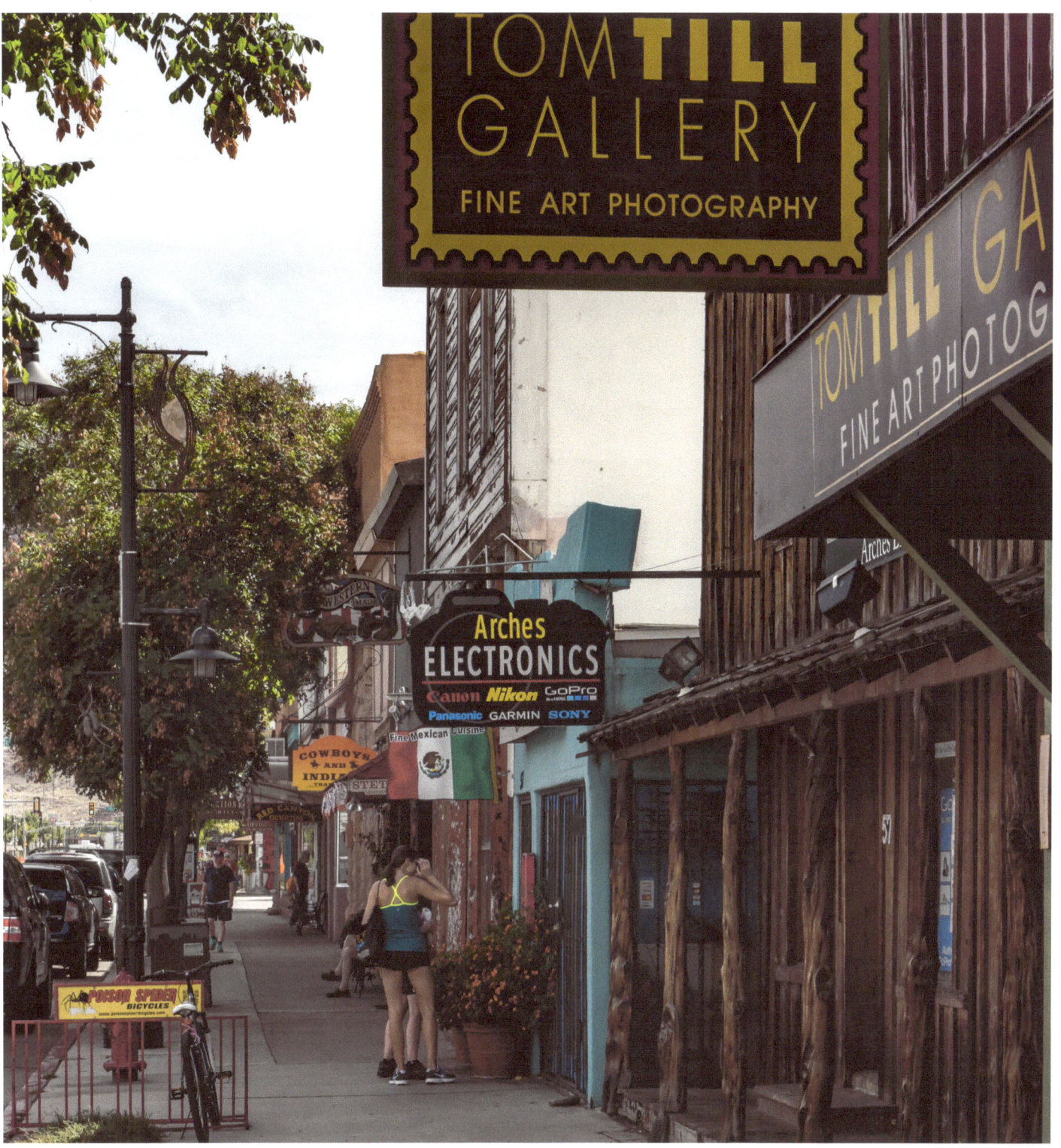

The town of Moab, Utah, is a great place to stay as you visit Arches, Canyonlands, Goblin Valley, Dead Horse Point, and Sego Canyon. Be sure to save a day just to look around Moab's shops, and stop by a restaurant or two.

Planning your Southwest Canyons Trip

Start with the essentials

Early in your planning process, consider the mode of transportation from your home to your destination airport. Because I wrote this book from the perspective of starting the road trip from the Las Vegas McCarran Airport, I'll assume that you are traveling by air from your home to the destination airport. The serious photographer might prefer to travel by personal vehicle in order to take more camera gear than air travel permits.

With air travel in mind, lay out each piece of luggage you will be allowed to take along (check with your airline to be sure). Next, lay out each item of clothing and gear you want to take along, including camera gear, and backpack(s).

Think about travel day(s) - what will you wear on the plane? This can be really important, especially if you think you might be close to the limit on luggage pieces and weight. By wearing some heavier items (hiking boots, for example), you will reduce your luggage weight.

If you are like me, this is the point where you start to make priority decisions. Should I take the big, heavy binoculars or extra hiking shorts and socks? You'll have to decide what really matters to you. Do bear in mind that many cheap everyday items can be purchased at a local store. Whatever is not used by the end of the trip can be put in the trash and forgotten.

Planning tip: Use a packing checklist

Make a checklist on your computer (I use Excel), so you don't forget anything. Include a section for things to do at home before you leave.

Do your Research

You may have purchased this book as a part of your planning, and if so, I thank you. I encourage readers to also go online to see other articles and photos from places discussed here and other nearby places. The southwest United States is rich with places like these. Make screen shots of the places you want to see, and print out the photos and descriptions to take along with you.

Planning tip: Create a Shot List

Photographers will benefit from a shot list, which I create in Excel prior to each photo trip. My way of creating a shot list is not the only way. I'll share just a few ideas you may want to incororate into your shot list.

As you do your research, for each location you find interesting, look it up in Google Maps. Zoom in close to see if you can determine where you want to view it, and possibly photograph it. Make a note in your shot list of the direction of the shot. Based on the direction of the shot, determine the best time of day for proper lighting.

Using this information, I have been able to optimize my planning for which places to visit on which days. You can only do one sunrise and one sunset each day, so planning out your shots will help you schedule where to be each day.

Of course, weather can always intervene. Be flexible and assume that some plans may not work out. The southwest is a big place!

Let's Calibrate Expectations

Many of the better-known canyons of the southwest have become immensely popular. For that reason, it is important to temper expectations before you travel.

I'll explain with an example. I once visited Mesa Arch in Canyonlands National Park on a weekday morning in late Fall. During planning, I failed to consider that a crowd might be there, despite my choice of a non-tourist travel date.

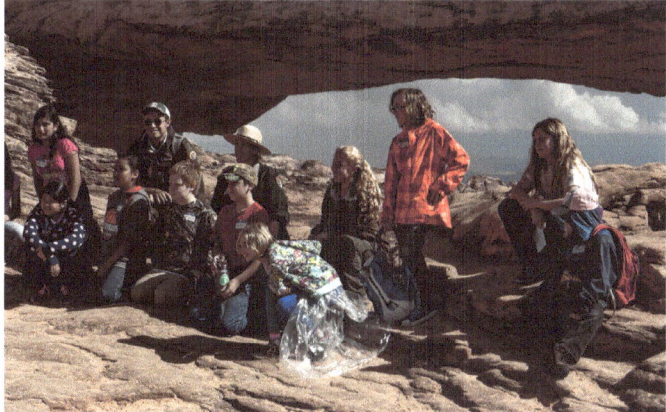

I have come to realize that each of us has the same right to get a photograph in a place like Mesa Arch, within a reasonable period of time. If, after hiking to a place you find a group there, there are usually several things you can be doing to prepare for your own shot of the scene when space opens up. One thing to do is take a few test shots, as I did (above).

That way, you won't have to fiddle around with such

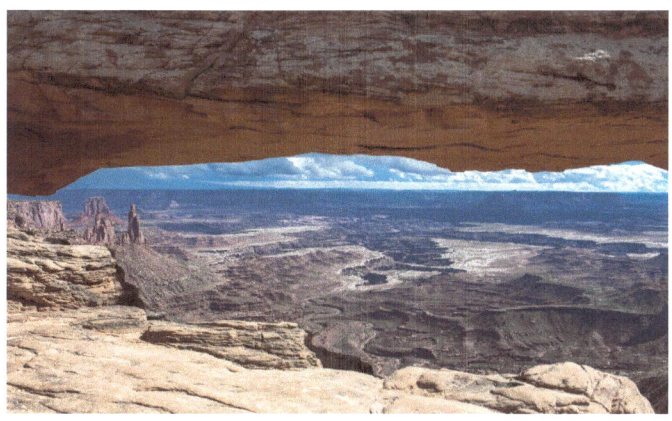

things as exposure settings and shutter speed when your chance comes.

For anyone reading this who is new to location photography, there are some common courtesies among photographers that may not be obvious. In the first example shot to the left, just after taking the test shot, another photographer walked behind the posed group, sizing up his shot through the arch. His action only slowed down the action, as the posing group waited for him to clear the background so they could get their shot.

Show courtesy for other photographers by looking to see if there is anyone behind you and to each side who may be trying to take a photo. Make sure the area is clear before walking around a scene like this. A bit of patience will pay off, and everyone will get a chance to get their shot.

One parting comment on this topic, and then I'll move on. You will encounter clueless people who will walk into your shot. You may find it tempting to say something nasty, but please don't do that. You will only leave a negative impression of all photographers by such an action.

Meet other Photographers and Ask Questions

This last suggestion may seem obvious, but it is something that did not come natural to me at first. Quite often after approaching someone at a location, I find out about another great location nearby or a detail about the history of a place only known to locals.

If you find the person knowledgeable and interesting, offer to exchange contact information. You may find that you have a friend who will help you the next time to return to the area. Give it a try!

The Artistry of *Wind, Water, & Time*

"I saw four angels standing at the four corners of the earth, holding back the four winds of the earth, that no wind might blow on earth or sea or against any tree."

Revelation 7:1

Wind

There are a number of examples in this book illustrating the role of wind in the creation of artistic formations in stone.

Long before any of the beautiful formations shown in this book existed, winds carried millions of tons of sand which were laid down across what is today the western United States. A long time later, large salt water oceans formed over the sands. The weight of the oceans compressed the sand into stone.

A long time after that, climate change occurred (similar to today), heating up the earth and drying almost all of the ocean. Great Salt Lake in Utah and the Salton Sea in California are present day saline lakes whose salt resulted from the drying of those earlier oceans.

Winds and rains next began to erode vast expanses of layers of sandstone across the southwest. Of course, wind erosion occurs over millions of years of time, and continues today. The hand of time is ever-present when we see the work of wind or water.

The curvacious walls of Lower and Upper Antelope Canyons have been carved primarily by wind. Occasional flash floods have happened, yes, but wind has always been present, and remains so.

Wild, lesser-known slot canyons scattered across Escalante and the Colorado River Plateau also display beautiful artistic lines and shapes to explore.

"Then the angel showed me the river of the water of life, bright as crystal, flowing from the throne of God and of the Lamb."

Revelation 22:1

Water

Water has been working on its canvas for millennia. Consider the Virgin River, flowing through Zion National Park. While the vertical canyon walls are not the work of the river, having been pushed up by geologic forces, the river has certainly carved its own artisitic channel through the idyllic canyon. A walk along the shores of the river is always a wonderful experience, but my favorite time of year is the Fall.

Bryce Canyon has no prominent water feature, and yet water has no doubt payed a major role in the erosion of layer upon layer of rock, each layer taking on a unque color and density characteristic, revealing high pinnacles of stone that survive today. Receding oceans, rainwater, and flooding over time have left us with the wonderland we call Bryce Canyon.

The winding Colorado River has shaped the landscape of Canyonlands National Park in a most dramatic way. As you drive along the national park road take time to stop at designated pullouts to take it all in.

Just outside of Canyonlands National Park lies Dead Horse Point State Park. This park is a jewel of geologic time. From the Visitor Center or the designated viewpoint, layer upon layer of stone, laid down over eons, paint the canvas in an array of colors. The river forms a 'Gooseneck' as it bends around the point and there is a special spot near the gooseneck that I would like to point out. Take a close look just to the left of the gooseneck in my photo of Dead Horse Point. Do you see the likeness of a large horse made of white capstone? That's amazing!

> *"But do not overlook this one fact, beloved, that with the Lord one day is as a thousand years, and a thousand years as one day."*
>
> 2 Peter 3:8

Time

Growing up as a child, I must have thought time is something that goes on forever. Perhaps it will. As I have gown older, I have confronted the certainty that these wonderful places that I photograph and write about will one day be completely gone - unrecognizable compared with what we see today. Wind, water and time will reduce the places we see today to sand and rubble.

A million years in the future, will mankind still be here, and will the records we create today enable our future brethren to see images of these places as we see them today? Delicate Arch will almost certainly be long forgotten then. Canyonlands might be deeper than the Grand Canyon, or perhaps collapsed into a pile of rubble. Bryce Canyon might be sand dunes, blowing across a desert landscape that we once called Utah.

Well, enough of that! Let's enjoy the wonderland we have today. Simply contemplating the preciousness of the present time raises my awareness of our fragile environment here on Earth.

You don't have to travel to exotic places to enjoy our wonderful planet. As a child, I received my first camera as a gift. I remember that camera well - it was a Kodak Brownie Starflash. I could take photos back then, but unlike today, I would have to wait at least a week to see them. And then, some of them might not have come out well, and I wished I had done a better job.

In those days, I would find things close to home to photograph. I liked butterflies, my dog, my cat, and my neighborhood friends as subjects.

Today is much the same. The vast majority of my collection of over 100,000 photos have been taken within a few miles of home. My neighborhood pond is a favorite place. Within a day's drive from my home in southwest Ohio, there is a national park, wildlife refuges, state parks known for waterfalls, and one of my favorite places, the northern Mississippi River, where I photograph migrating bald eagles each January and February. What wonderful things are close to you?

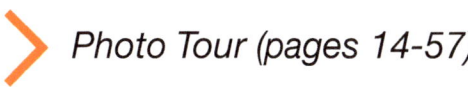

Photo Tour (pages 14-57)

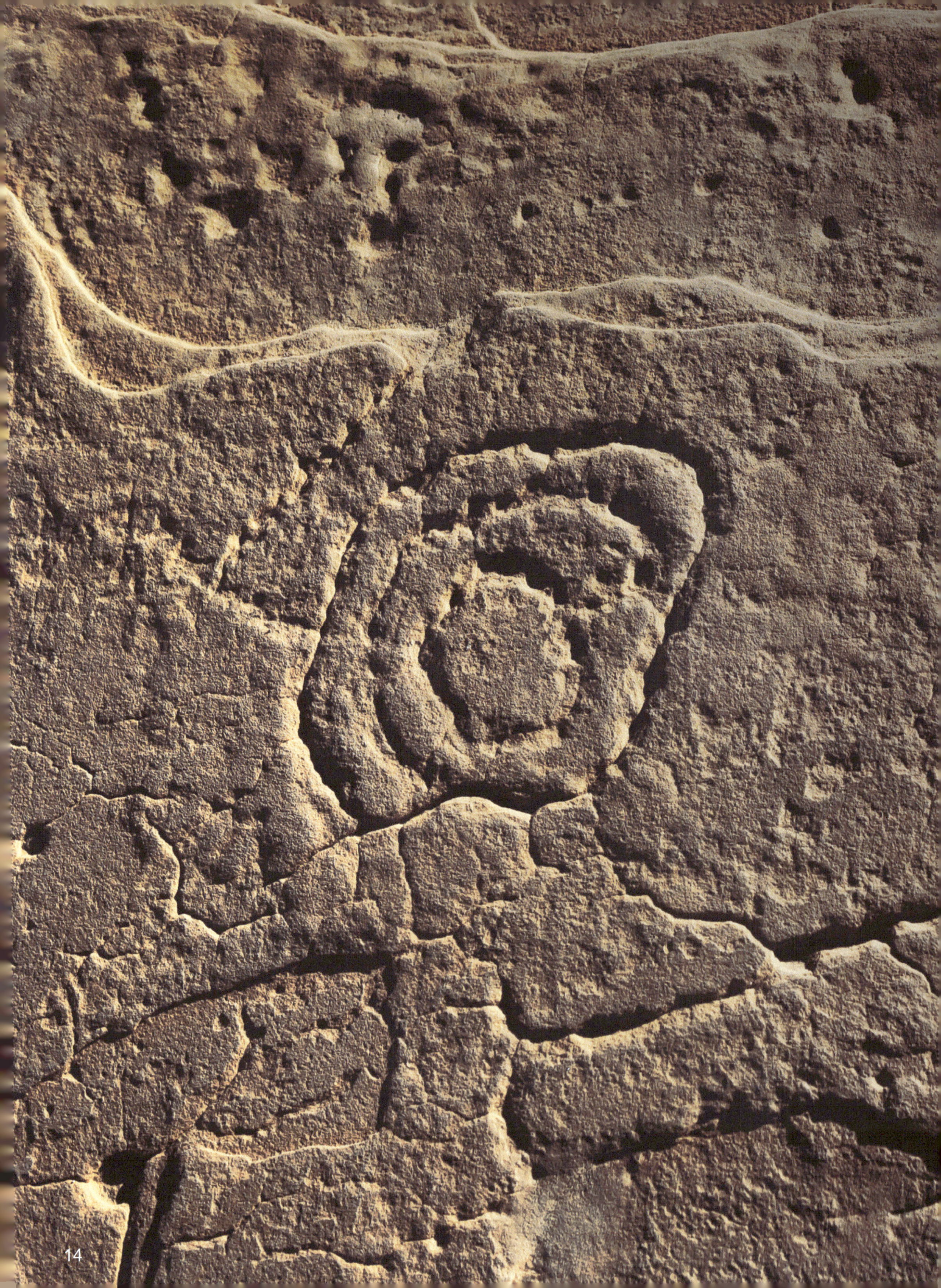

VALLEY OF FIRE
STATE PARK, NEVADA

As I was departing Las Vegas McCarran International Airport, driving to Zion National Park, I noticed a 'points-of-interest' sign for Valley of Fire State Park.

Checking my watch, I decided to turn off to check the place out. I am glad I did!

This site has some of the most ancient signs of early man that I have personally witnessed. Let me admit right now that I am no expert on anthropology or archeology, but I do stop to read what is displayed at archeological sites.

Valley of Fire State Park has a visitor center, and there you will find relevant archeological information about the rock formations as well as ancient people who have lived in the area over the past two thousand years.

Footprints of the ancients?

I invite you look closely at the left side of this 2-page spread (page 14). This is a horizontal sandstone formation (rock art is usually found on vertical surfaces or standing stones). This art cannot be seen from ground level. I saw it only after climbing on top, and I shot it looking straight down onto the horizontal surface. The last time I visited, the area was marked, 'No climbing.'

About half-way down and in the center of the page, you will see three concentric circles, possibly a symbol for the sun.

Just below the circles and slightly left, you will see a possible impression left when an ancient artist stood in soft sandy clay while drawing.

The remaining art appears to have been created by drawing with a stick or sharp rock in sandy clay soil. One theory is this sandy soil or beach existed alongside an ancient lake, created as seas dried up thousands of years ago.

With the passage of time, and the heat of desert sun, this section of sandy beach hardened into stone.

This particular rock art is the only example of drawing in soft material I have ever found. It is one of the most fascinating examples of rock art that I have seen.

Arch Rock
Valley of Fire State Park, AZ

The photos on this page were all taken within a few hundred feet of the car. For those so inclined, you will get great shots without long, strenuous hikes.

That said, I have no doubt that even better images can ge had if one is willing to spend more time and energy looking for them.

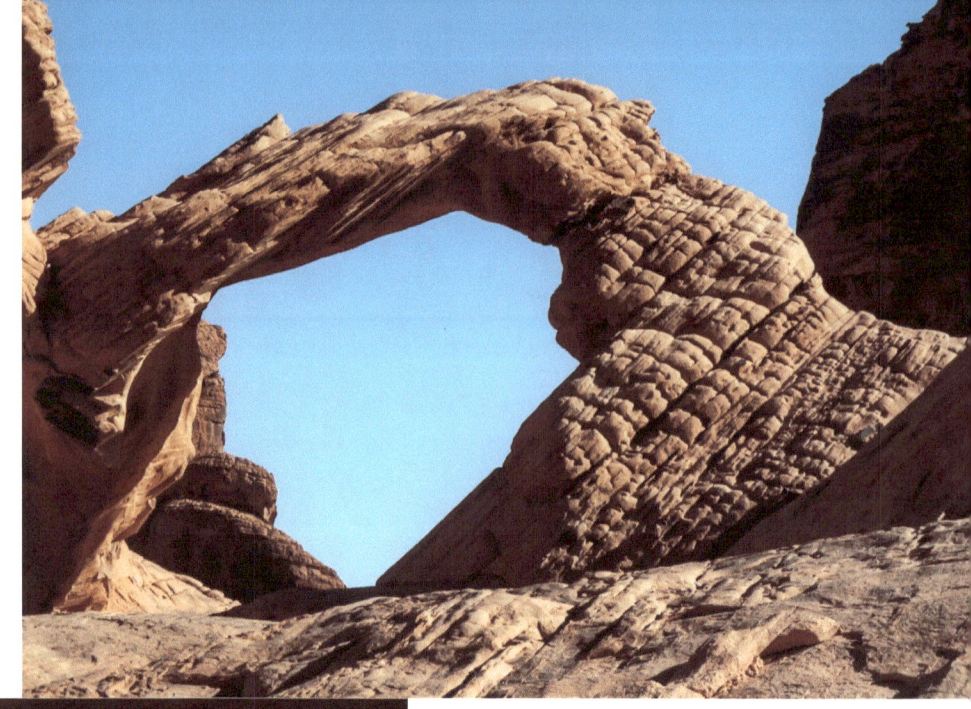

Sandstone Cave
Valley of Fire State Park, AZ

Looking back on my brief visits to Valley of Fire, I now wish I had allotted more time to the site.

This sandstone cave is just one example of a site that is worth more investigation. Not visible in the photo, there is a small inscription in one of the walls where it appears someone long ago was counting something... days, baskets of grain?

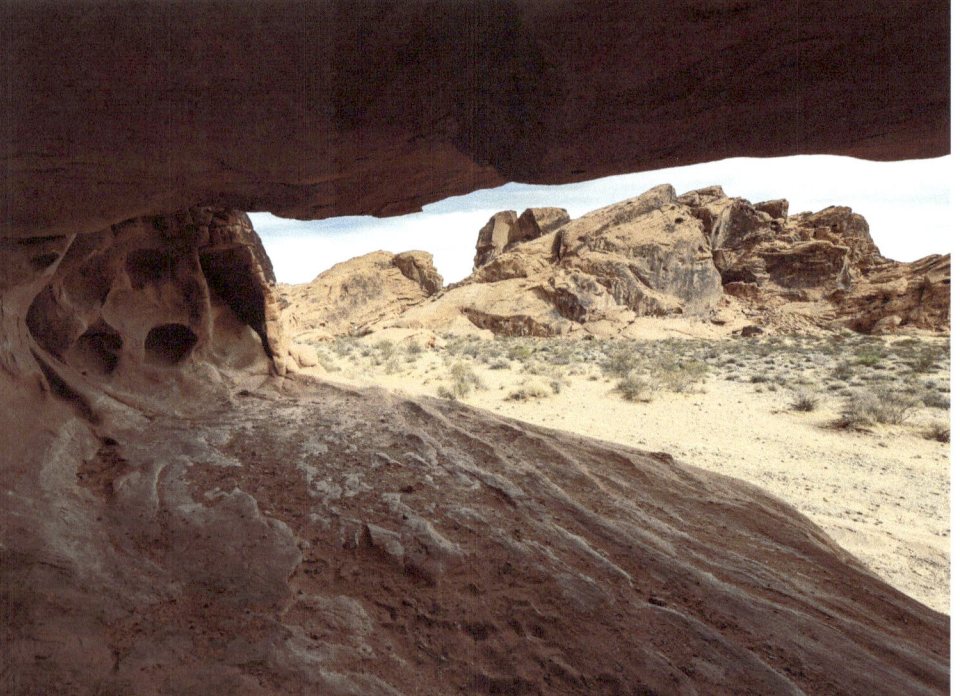

Petrified Sand Dune
Valley of Fire State Park, AZ

These sandstone formations can be found in many locations around the southwest. My understanding is that a vast sandy desert was once laid down by wind across the southwest, then compressed by massive seas which, over time, dried up, leaving behind many interesting formations. It took wind, water, and time to create.

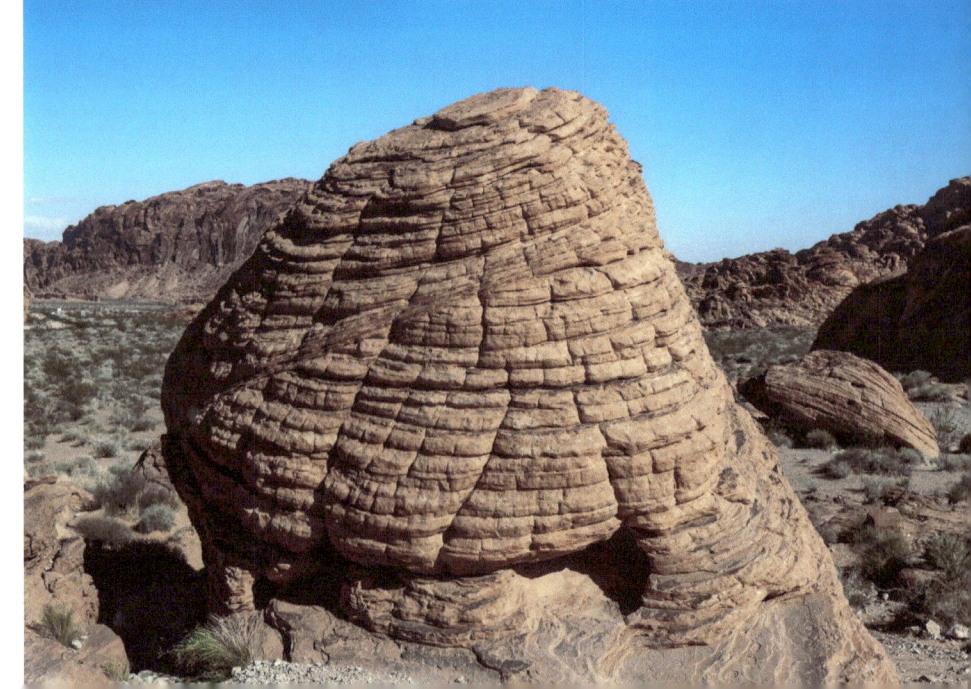

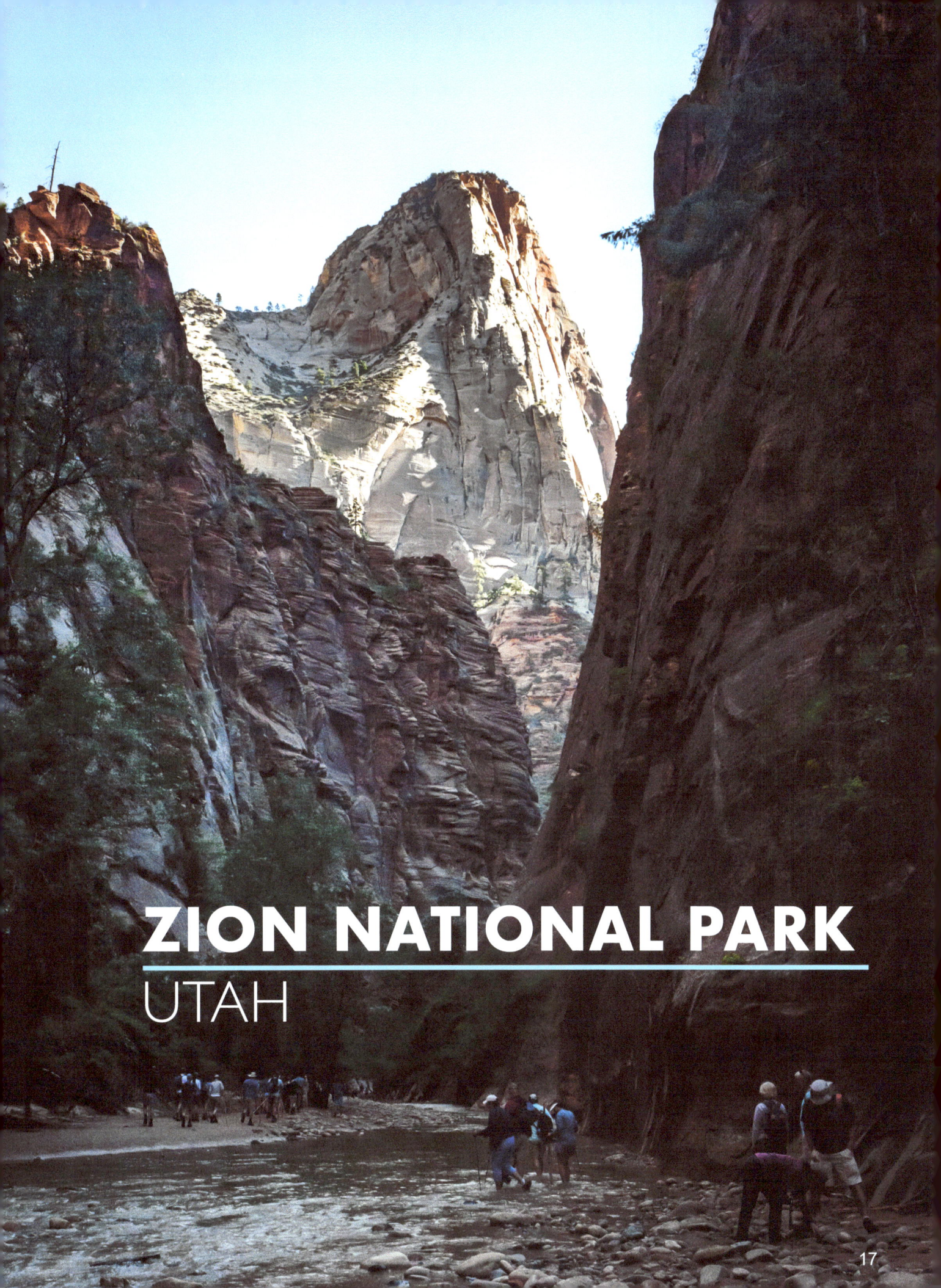
ZION NATIONAL PARK
UTAH

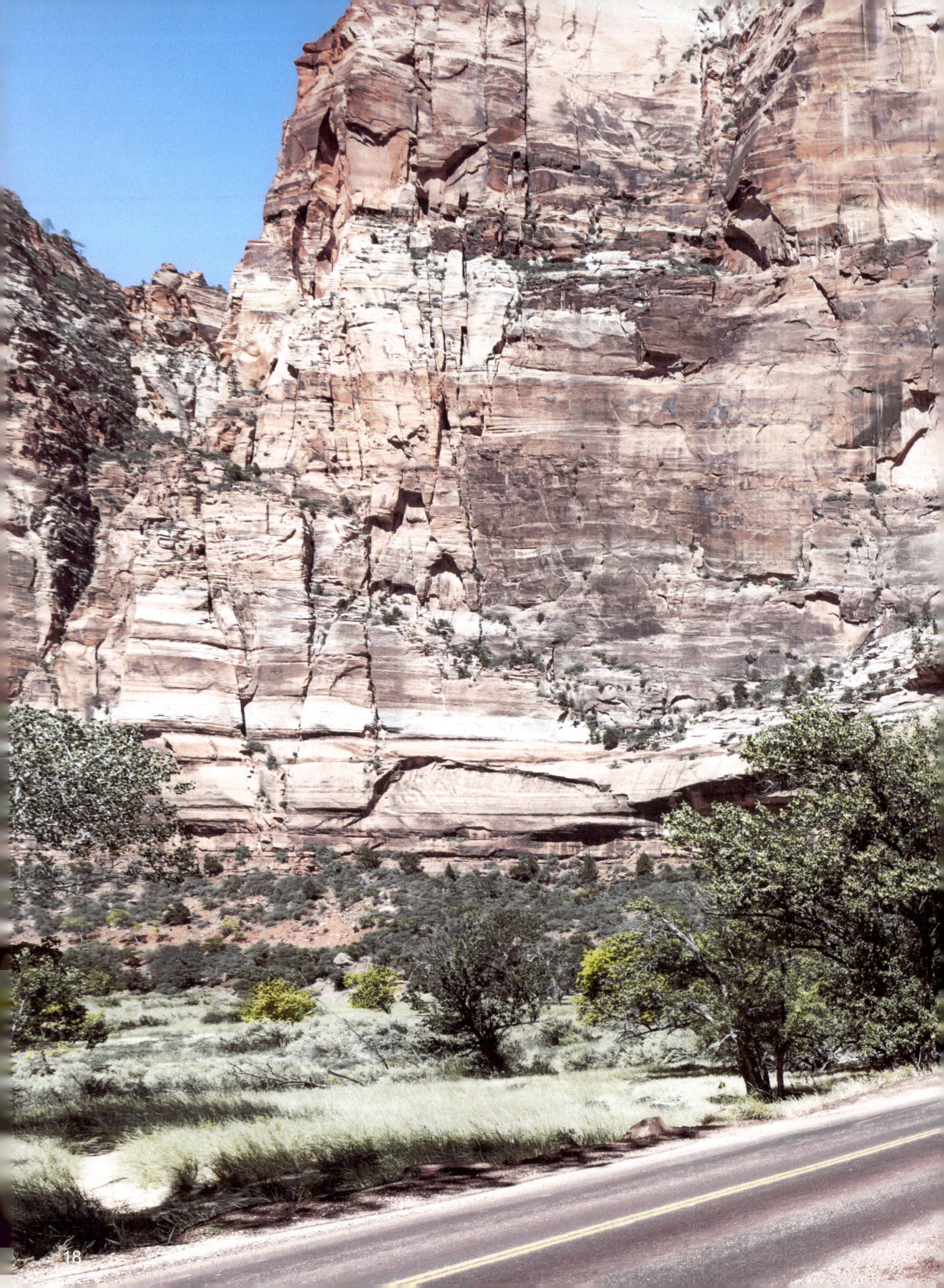

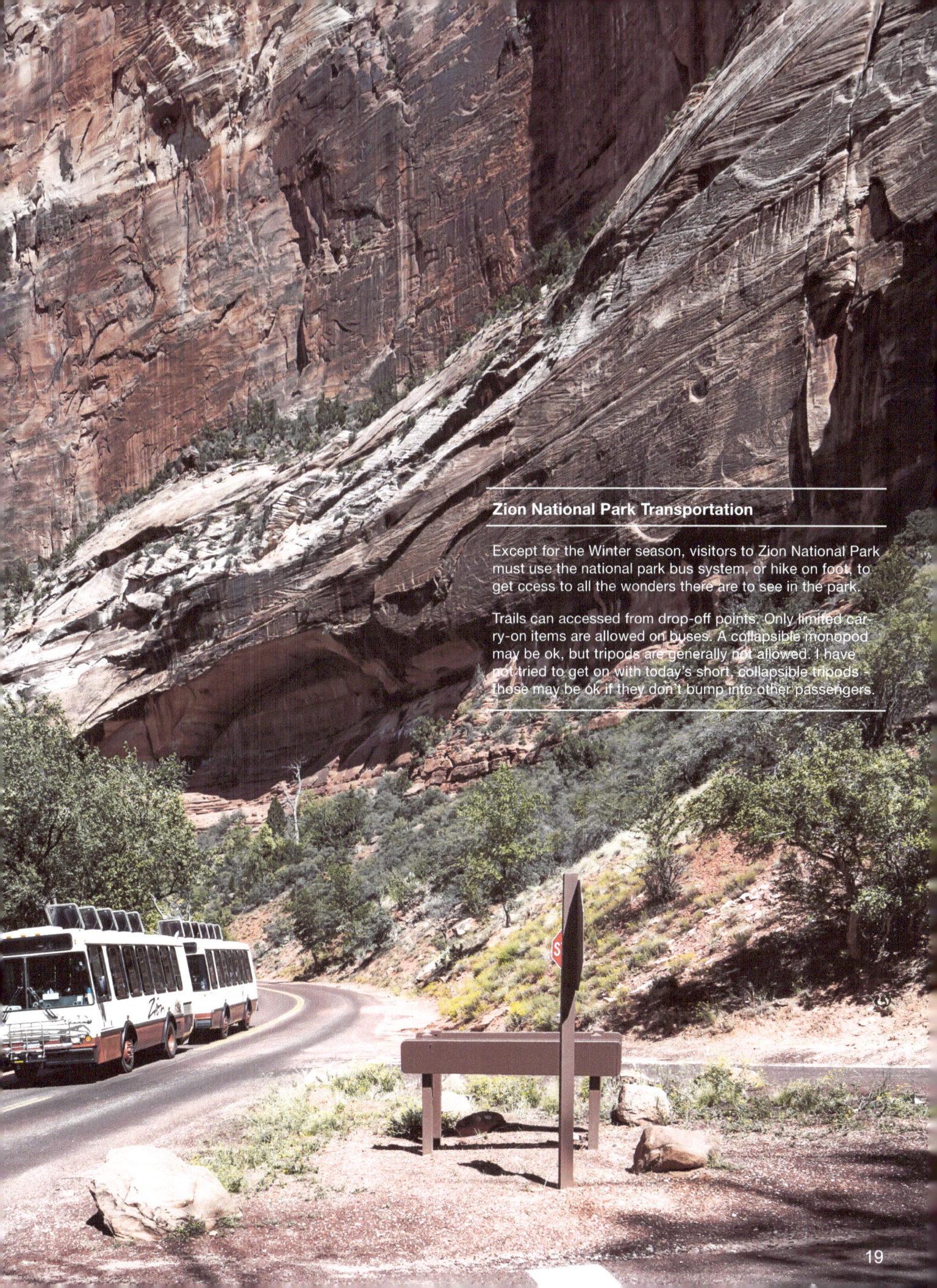

Zion National Park Transportation

Except for the Winter season, visitors to Zion National Park must use the national park bus system, or hike on foot, to get ccess to all the wonders there are to see in the park.

Trails can accessed from drop-off points. Only limited carry-on items are allowed on buses. A collapsible monopod may be ok, but tripods are generally not allowed. I have not tried to get on with today's short, collapsible tripods - those may be ok if they don't bump into other passengers.

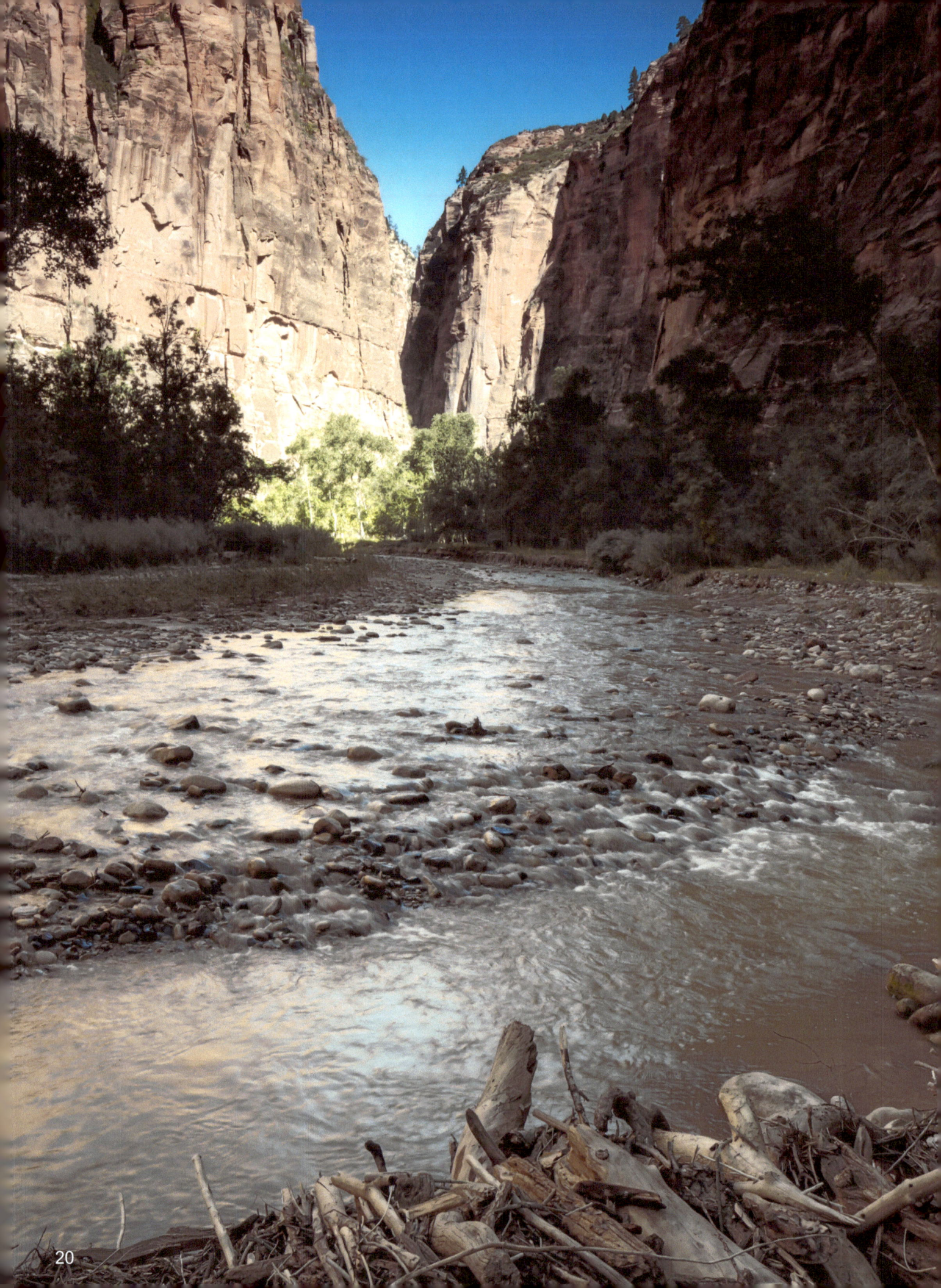

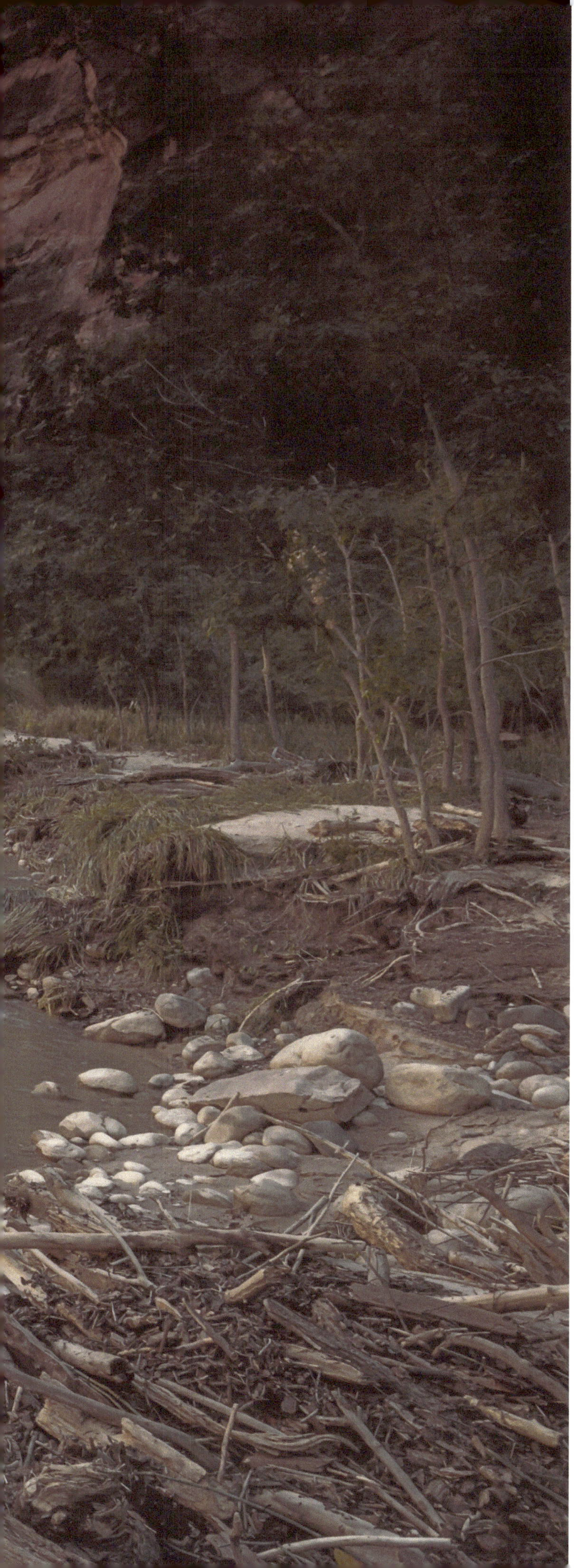

What to Expect on your Zion Visit

The first thing to consider when planning a trip to Zion is the park policy restricting private vehicle access to the park, except during the winter season.

This is important if you plan to do any sort of photography that will require a sturdy tripod or more equipment than you can carry aboard a crowded tour bus. In the event that you will travel during the more popular tourist seasons, all is not lost. You will have ample opportunities to get off the bus at stops along the route.

Trails are marked from bus stops to various points of interest. Trail difficulty ranges from easily walked trails alongside the Virgin River canyon to difficult hikes with significant elevation change. Some hikes will involve getting wet, such as a hike through 'The Narrows.'

> **Tech Tips:**
>
> Photographers using DSLR and advanced mirrorless cameras may consider carrying a graduated neutral density filter set. Many locations along the Virgin River canyon will present striking scenes of canyon walls that will appear much darker than the bright sky above. A graduated neutral density filter will compensate for the high contrast between these areas of your images, making processing of your digital files much less challenging.
>
> Remember to turn your camera so that you get portrait orientation (vertical) shots too. Many of Zion's best scenes are those featuring towering canyon walls set against white stone formations in the distance, and dramatic blue sky most of the time. While it is possible to crop your landscape (horiontal) shots to a vertical shape, cropped images lose much of the native resolution of the image, resulting in a final image that lacks the clarity of an uncropped image shot vertically.

Left:
Virgin River, Zion Canyon

Previous, pages 18-19:
NPS Bus, Zion Canyon Scenic Drive

Previous, page 17:
Virgin River, Zion Canyon

Next, pages 22-23:
'The Grotto'

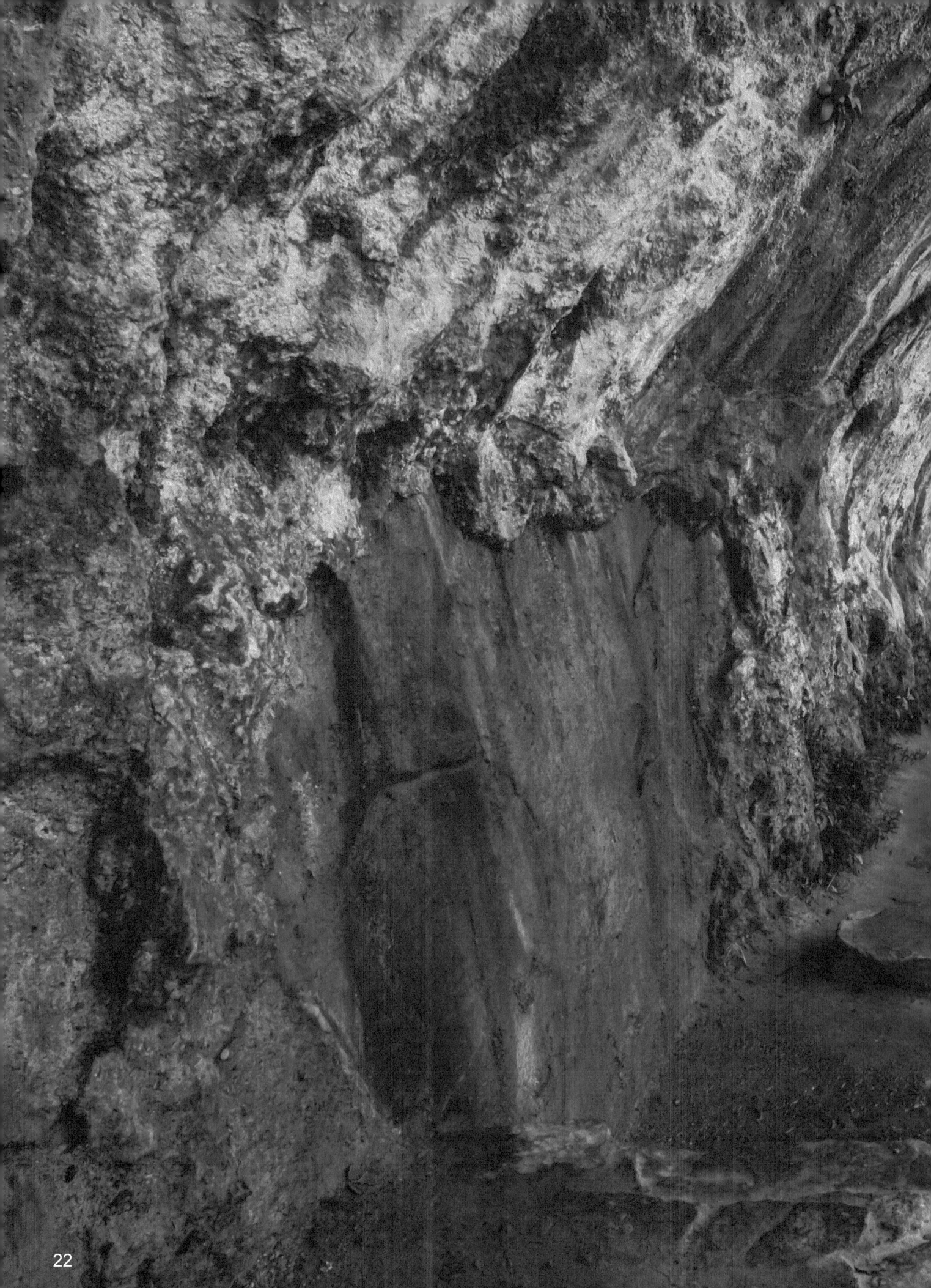

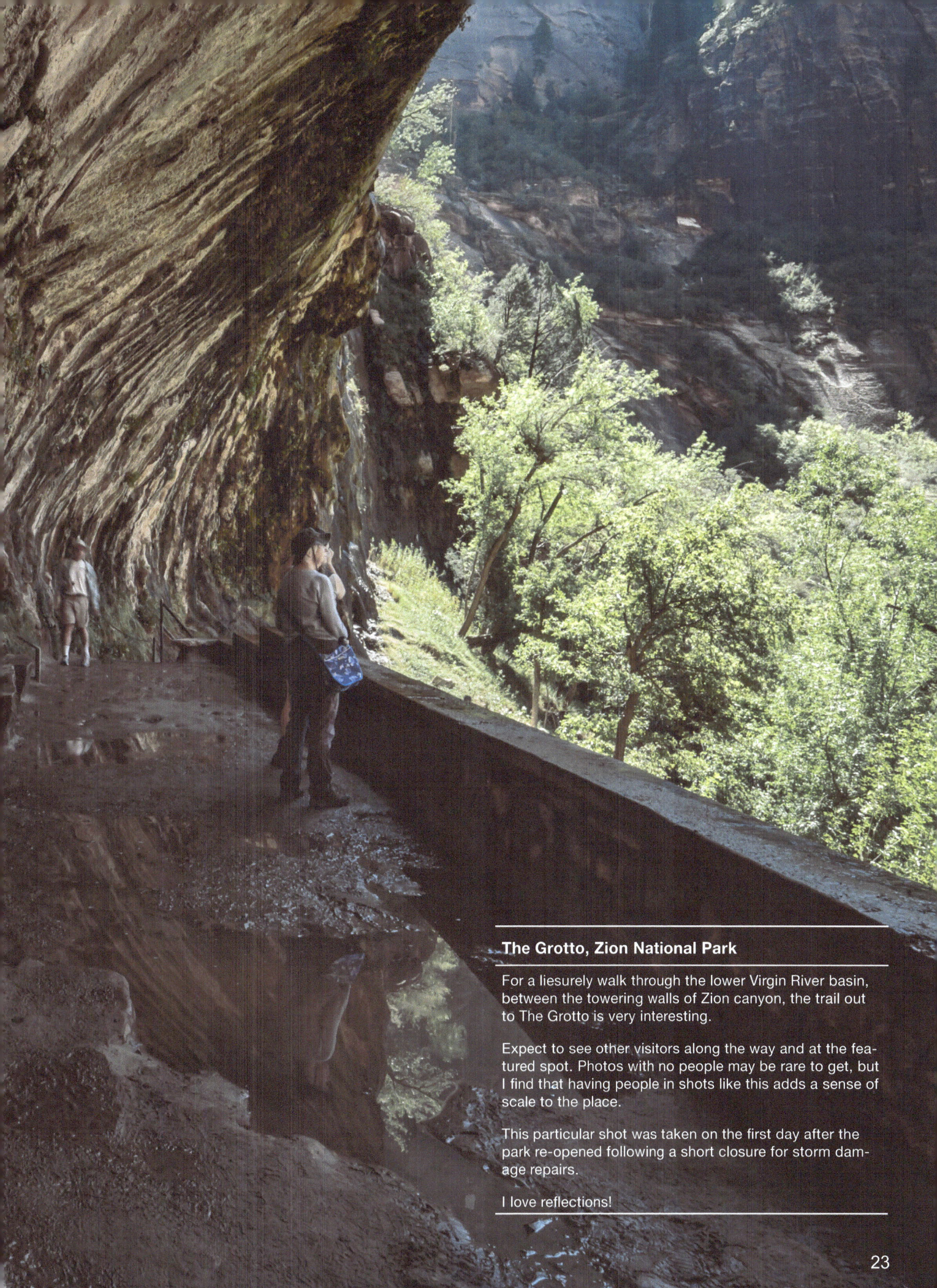

The Grotto, Zion National Park

For a liesurely walk through the lower Virgin River basin, between the towering walls of Zion canyon, the trail out to The Grotto is very interesting.

Expect to see other visitors along the way and at the featured spot. Photos with no people may be rare to get, but I find that having people in shots like this adds a sense of scale to the place.

This particular shot was taken on the first day after the park re-opened following a short closure for storm damage repairs.

I love reflections!

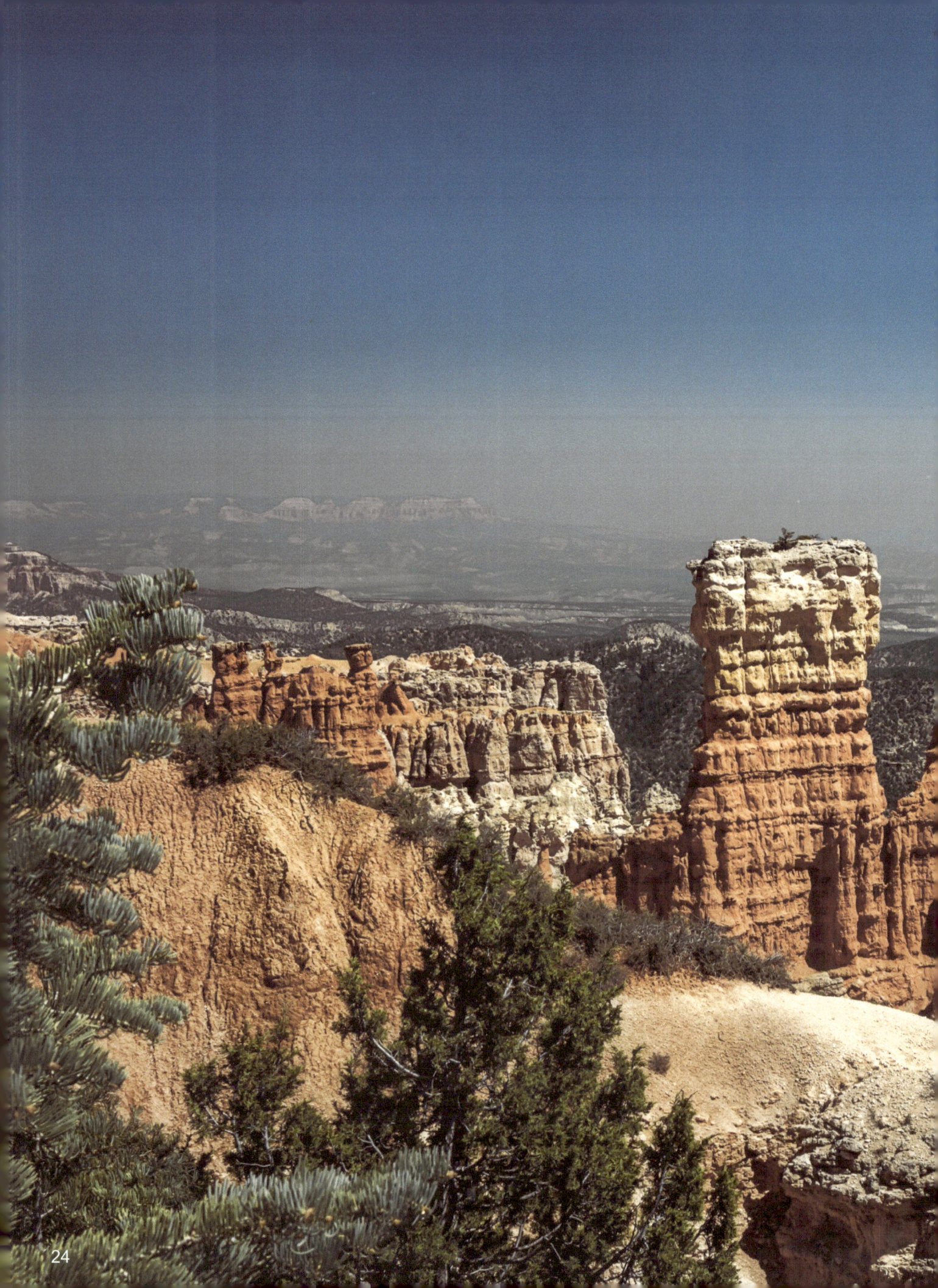

BRYCE CANYON
NATIONAL PARK, UTAH

My first visit to Bryce Canyon was unforgettable and somewhat unique, as canyons go. As I first approached the national park by car, I was surprised to find myself looking down into deep chasms filled with bright orange spikes rising up to my level and higher.

Most of my prior experience photographing canyons of the southwest had been done from the canyon floor, framing vertical shots and dealing with dark canyon walls contrasted with bright skies.

In Bryce Canyon, by comparison, much of my photography has been done from vistas high above the canyon floor. You may find your creativity limited by only seeing this magnificent park from the vista parking areas, so I encourage you to find alternate locations.

Driving through the park on the first day, scouting the area to get a sense of its overall layout, I took note of interesting views from above, of course, but I also began to locate trails that would take me from the upper vistas down into lower levels of the canyon, between sandstone pillars. I did not want to limit myself to the same scenes that everyone else gets.

One location I found interesting is called Navajo Loop Trail. Be sure to get a park map at the entrance.

Before you depart on one of the trails that take you into the lower reaches of the canyon, be aware that you will be dealing with steep sections and significant elevation changes. Take your time, rest often, and drink water!

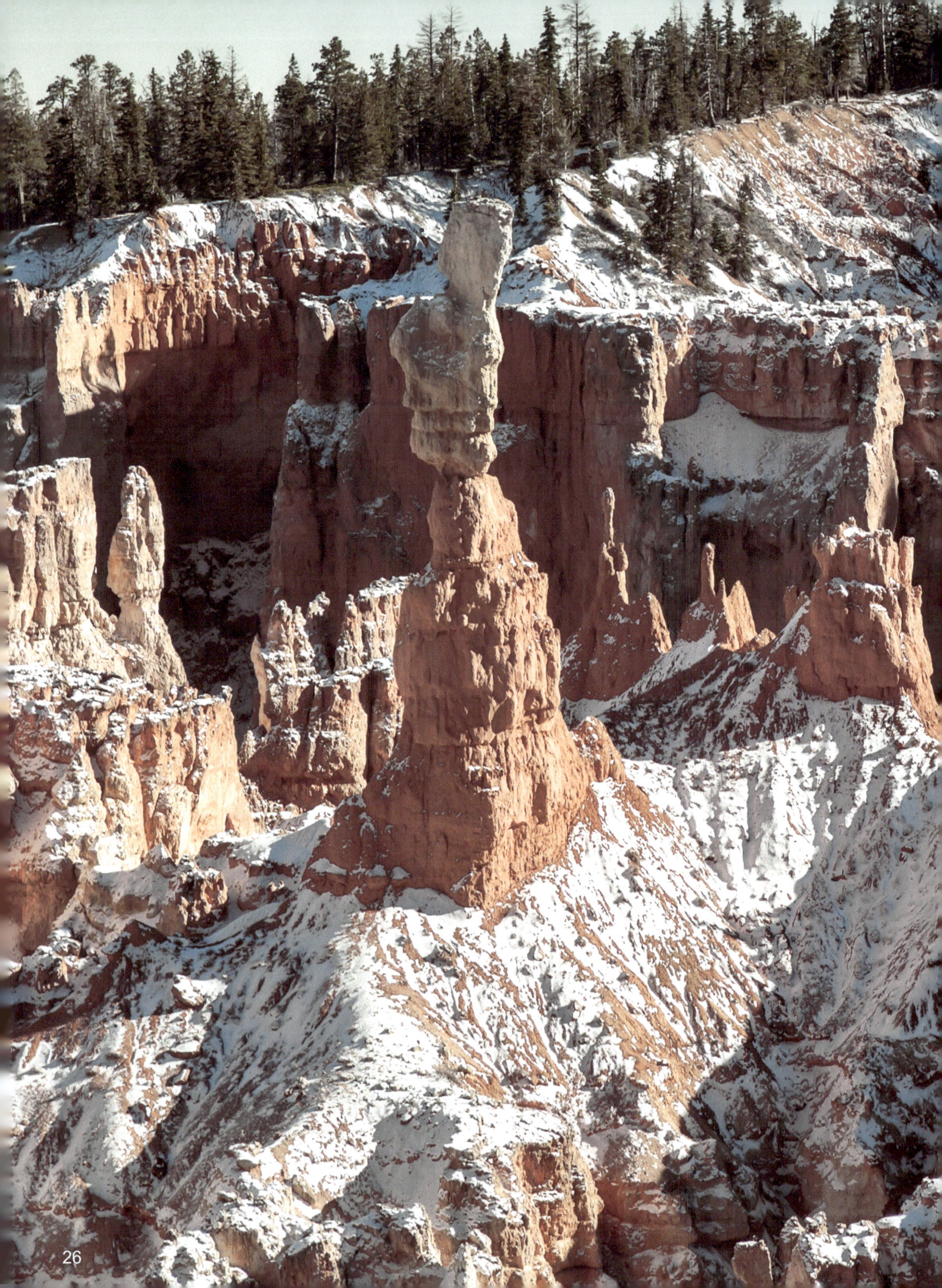

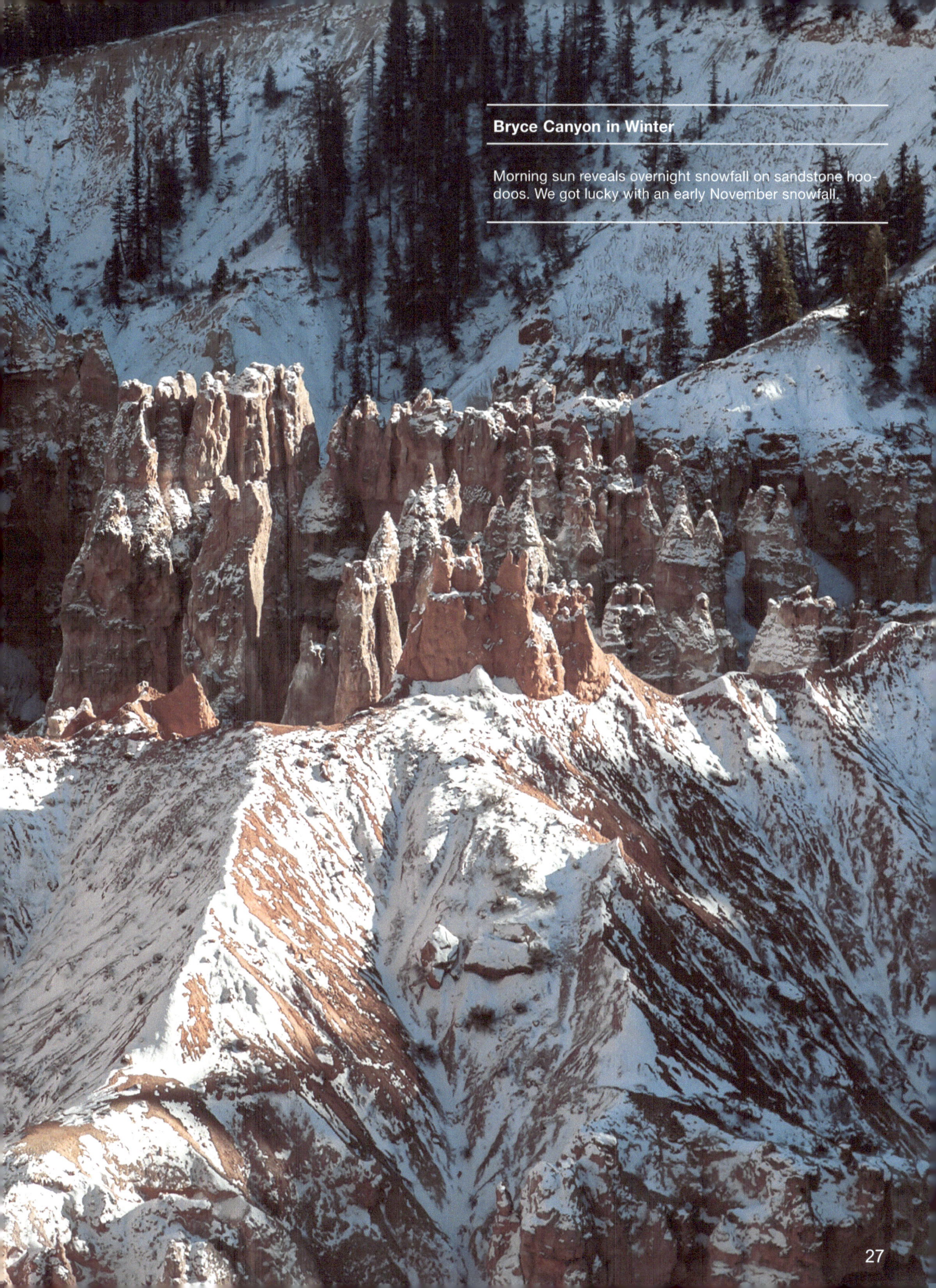

Bryce Canyon in Winter

Morning sun reveals overnight snowfall on sandstone hoodoos. We got lucky with an early November snowfall.

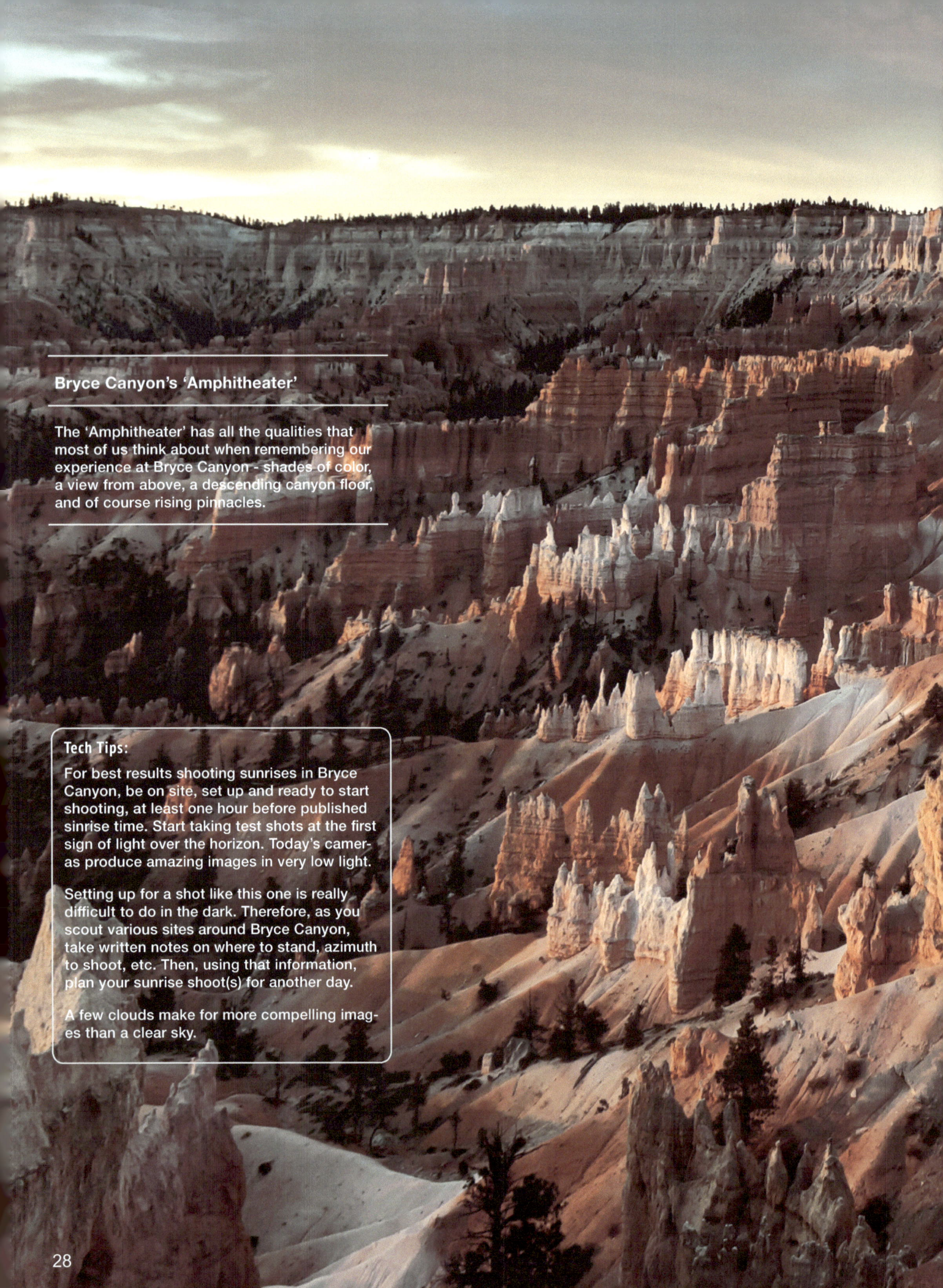

Bryce Canyon's 'Amphitheater'

The 'Amphitheater' has all the qualities that most of us think about when remembering our experience at Bryce Canyon - shades of color, a view from above, a descending canyon floor, and of course rising pinnacles.

Tech Tips:

For best results shooting sunrises in Bryce Canyon, be on site, set up and ready to start shooting, at least one hour before published sinrise time. Start taking test shots at the first sign of light over the horizon. Today's cameras produce amazing images in very low light.

Setting up for a shot like this one is really difficult to do in the dark. Therefore, as you scout various sites around Bryce Canyon, take written notes on where to stand, azimuth to shoot, etc. Then, using that information, plan your sunrise shoot(s) for another day.

A few clouds make for more compelling images than a clear sky.

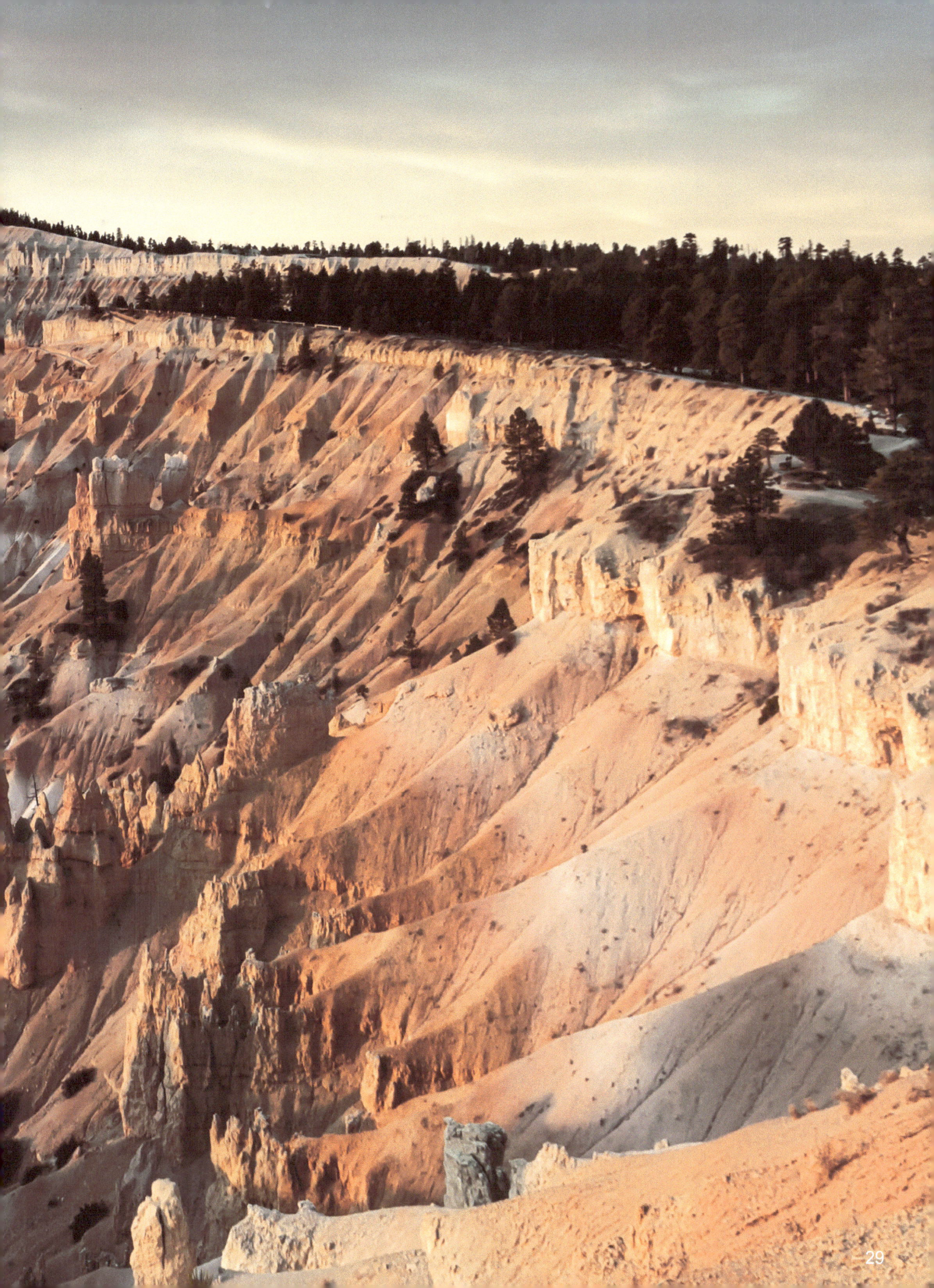

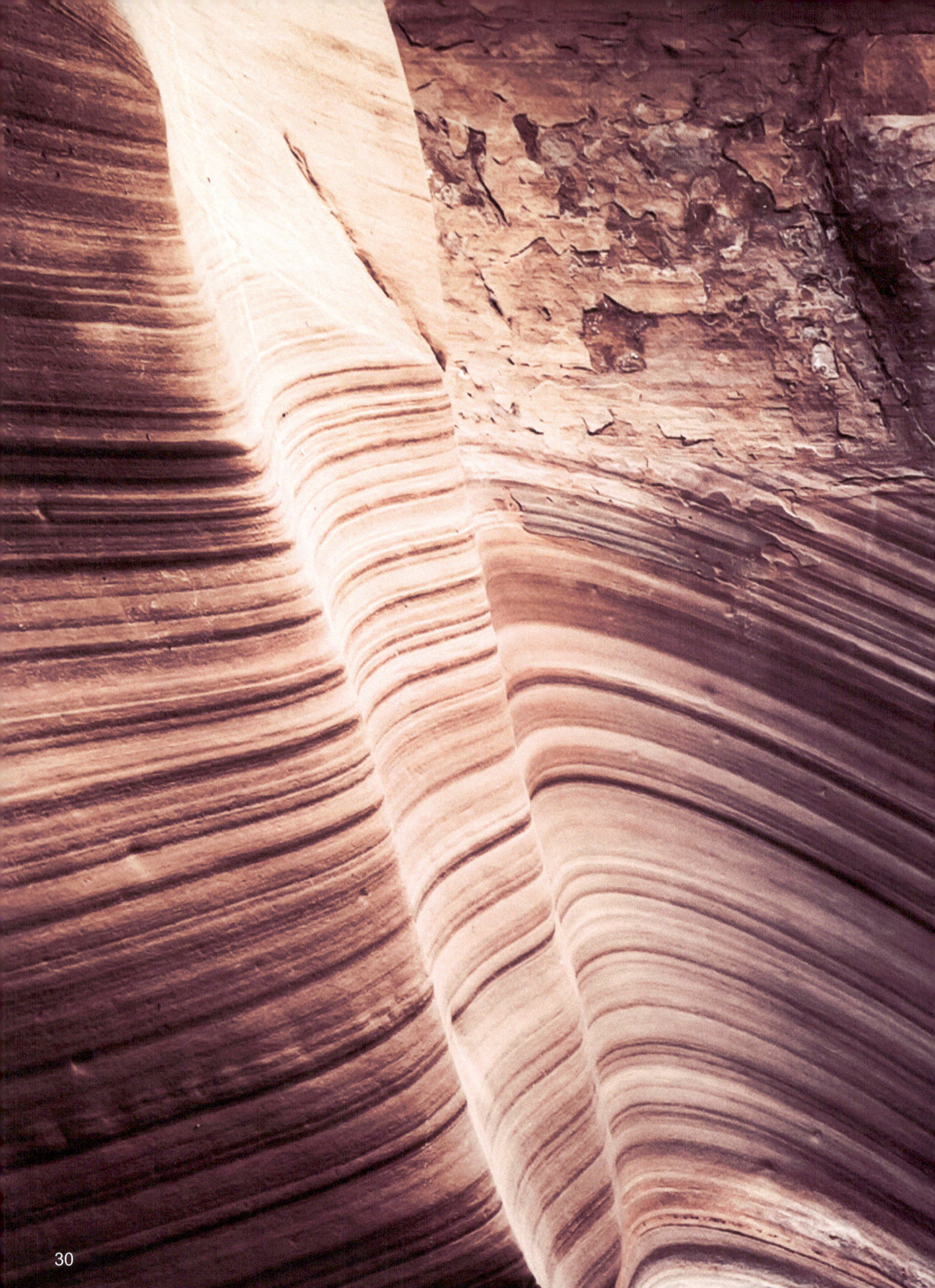

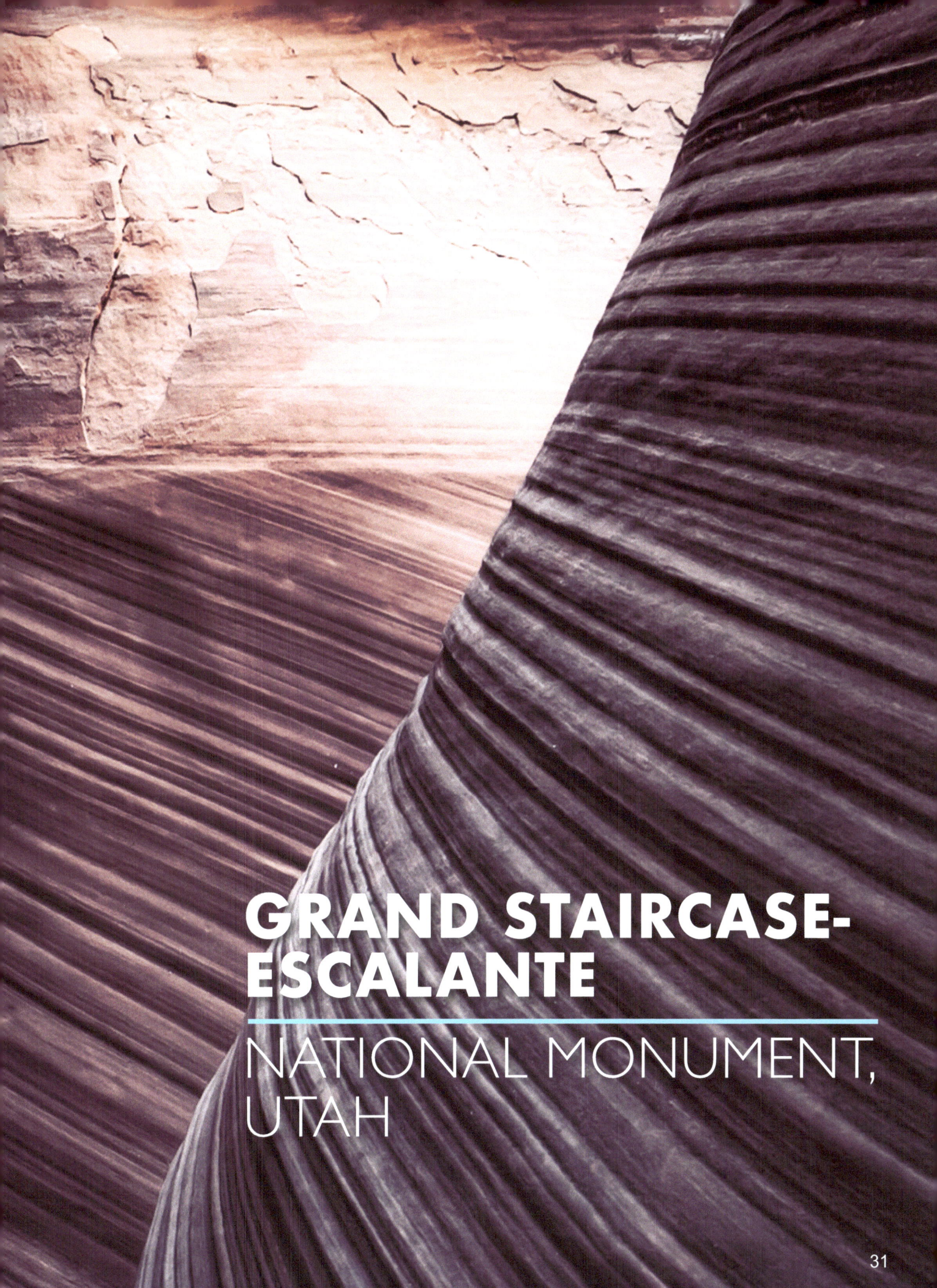

GRAND STAIRCASE-ESCALANTE

NATIONAL MONUMENT, UTAH

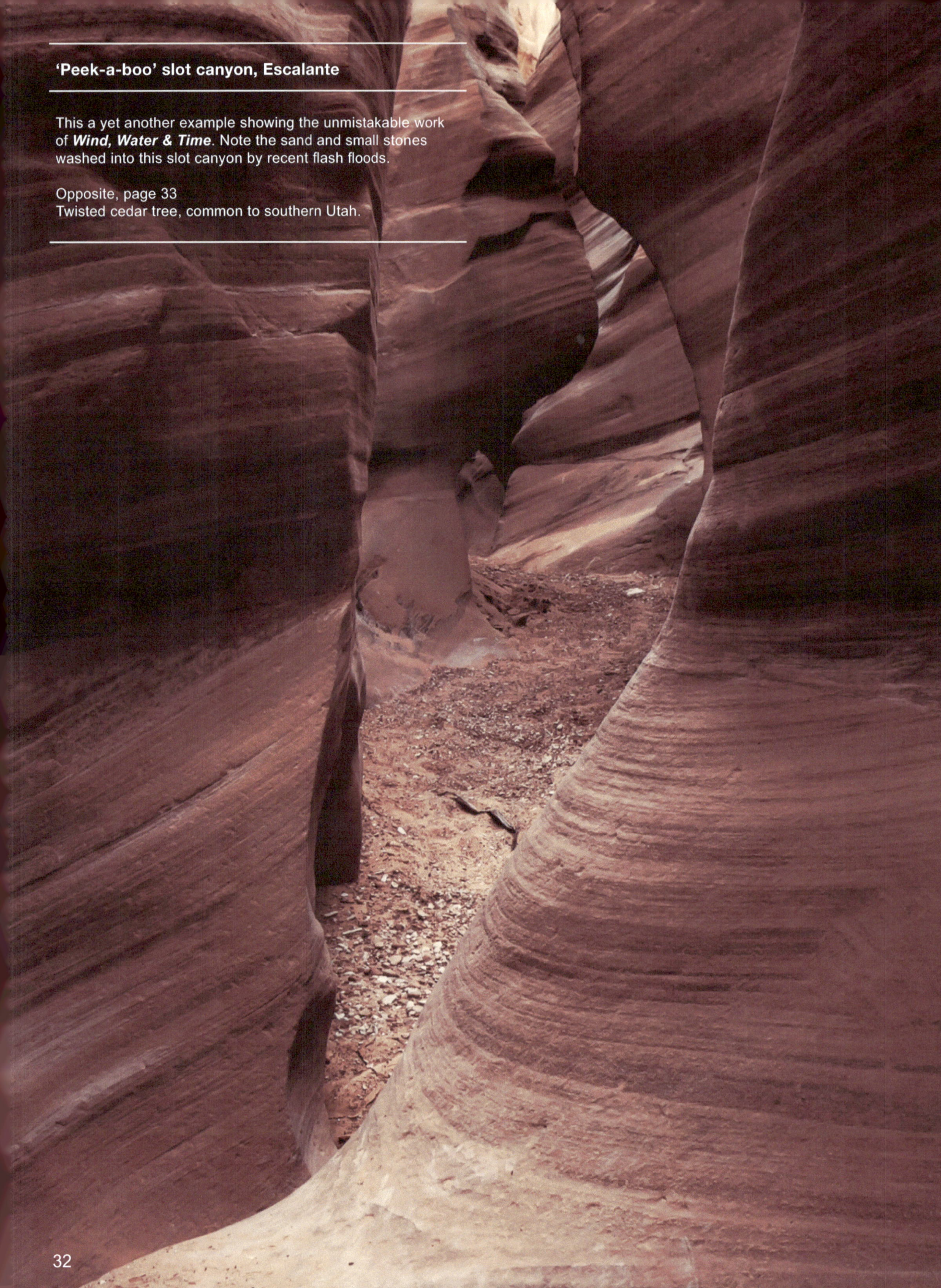

'Peek-a-boo' slot canyon, Escalante

This a yet another example showing the unmistakable work of **Wind, Water & Time**. Note the sand and small stones washed into this slot canyon by recent flash floods.

Opposite, page 33
Twisted cedar tree, common to southern Utah.

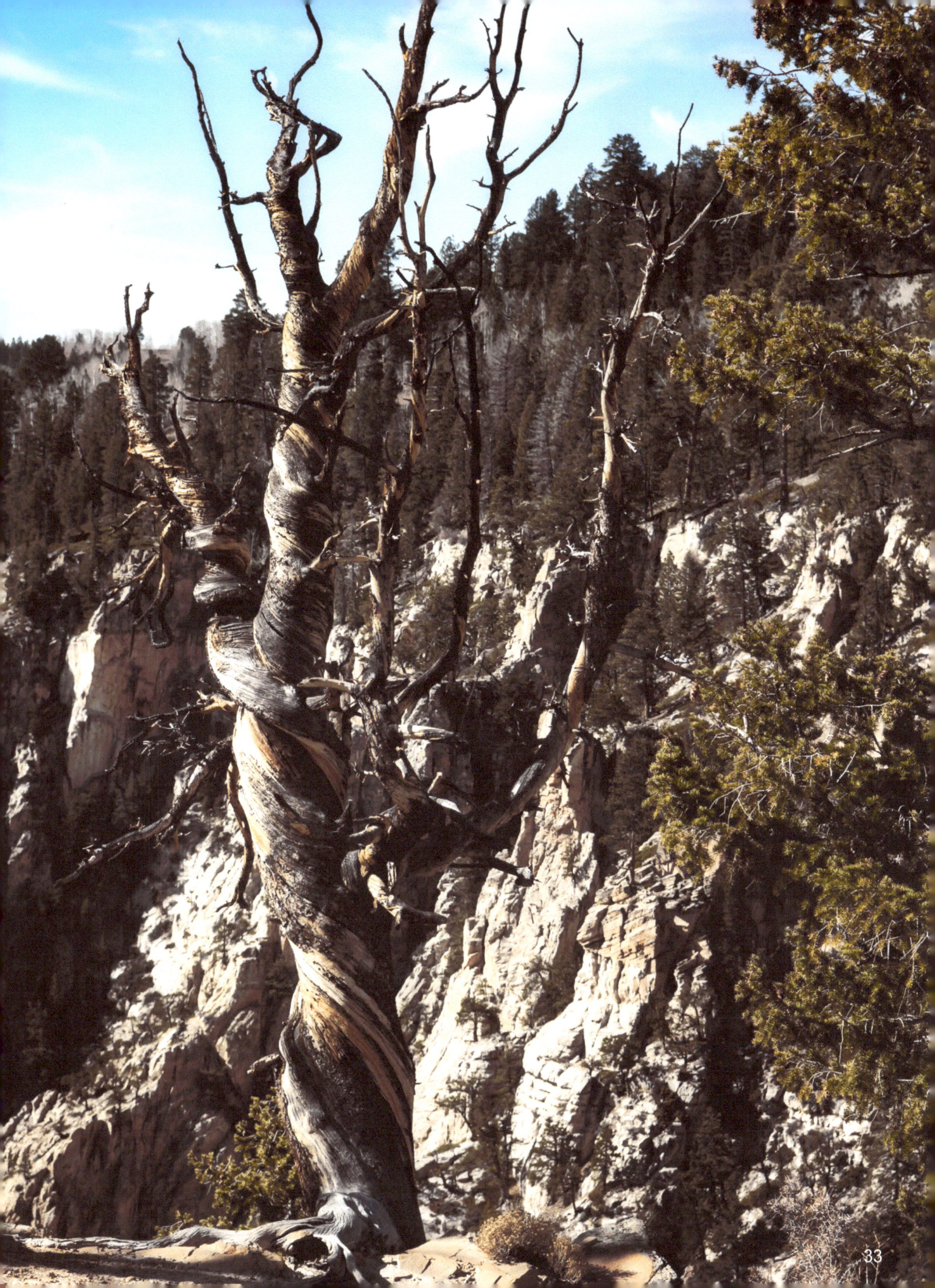

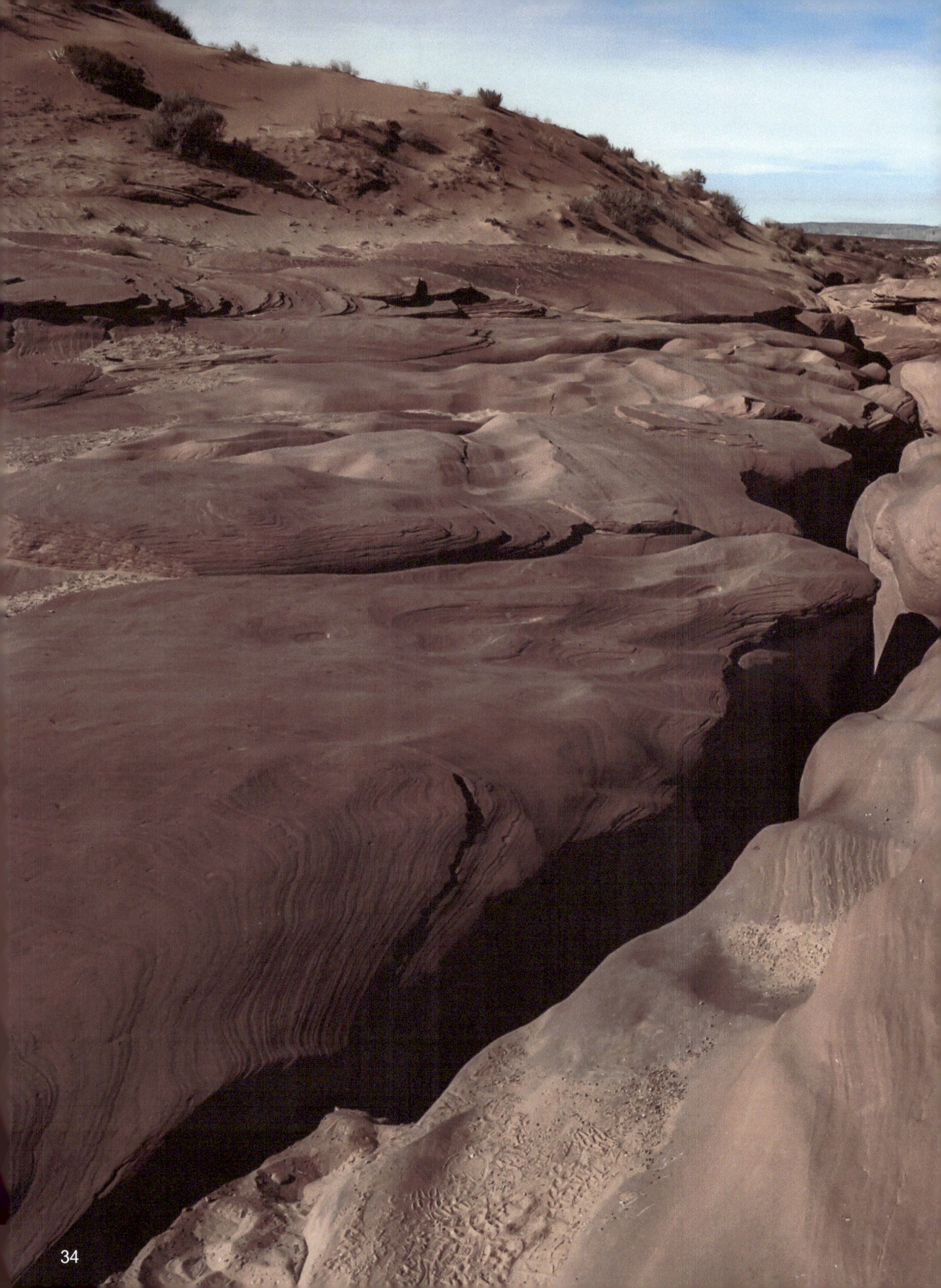

ANTELOPE CANYON
NAVAJO PARK, ARIZONA

Lower Antelope Canyon, Page AZ

On my first visit, after registering and starting the walk out to the canyon, I grew concerned that I had made a mistake. Could this be the famous deep slot canyon with flaming colors? It looked like a crack in the ground!

Notice the footprints in the sand (lower left)? That's where you enter, if your tour starts at the south end. From there, the floor will drop 120 feet by the time you reach the far end.

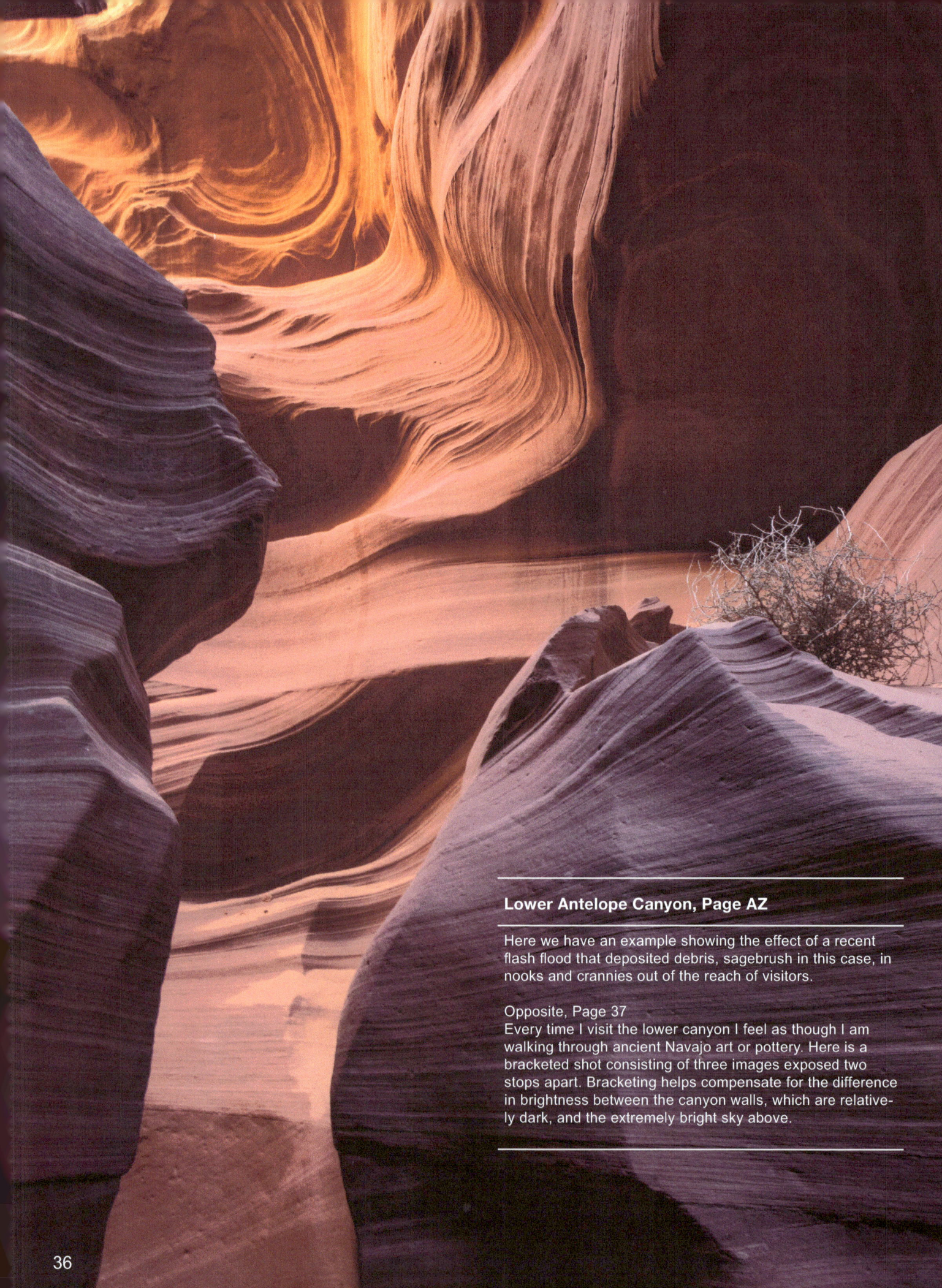

Lower Antelope Canyon, Page AZ

Here we have an example showing the effect of a recent flash flood that deposited debris, sagebrush in this case, in nooks and crannies out of the reach of visitors.

Opposite, Page 37
Every time I visit the lower canyon I feel as though I am walking through ancient Navajo art or pottery. Here is a bracketed shot consisting of three images exposed two stops apart. Bracketing helps compensate for the difference in brightness between the canyon walls, which are relatively dark, and the extremely bright sky above.

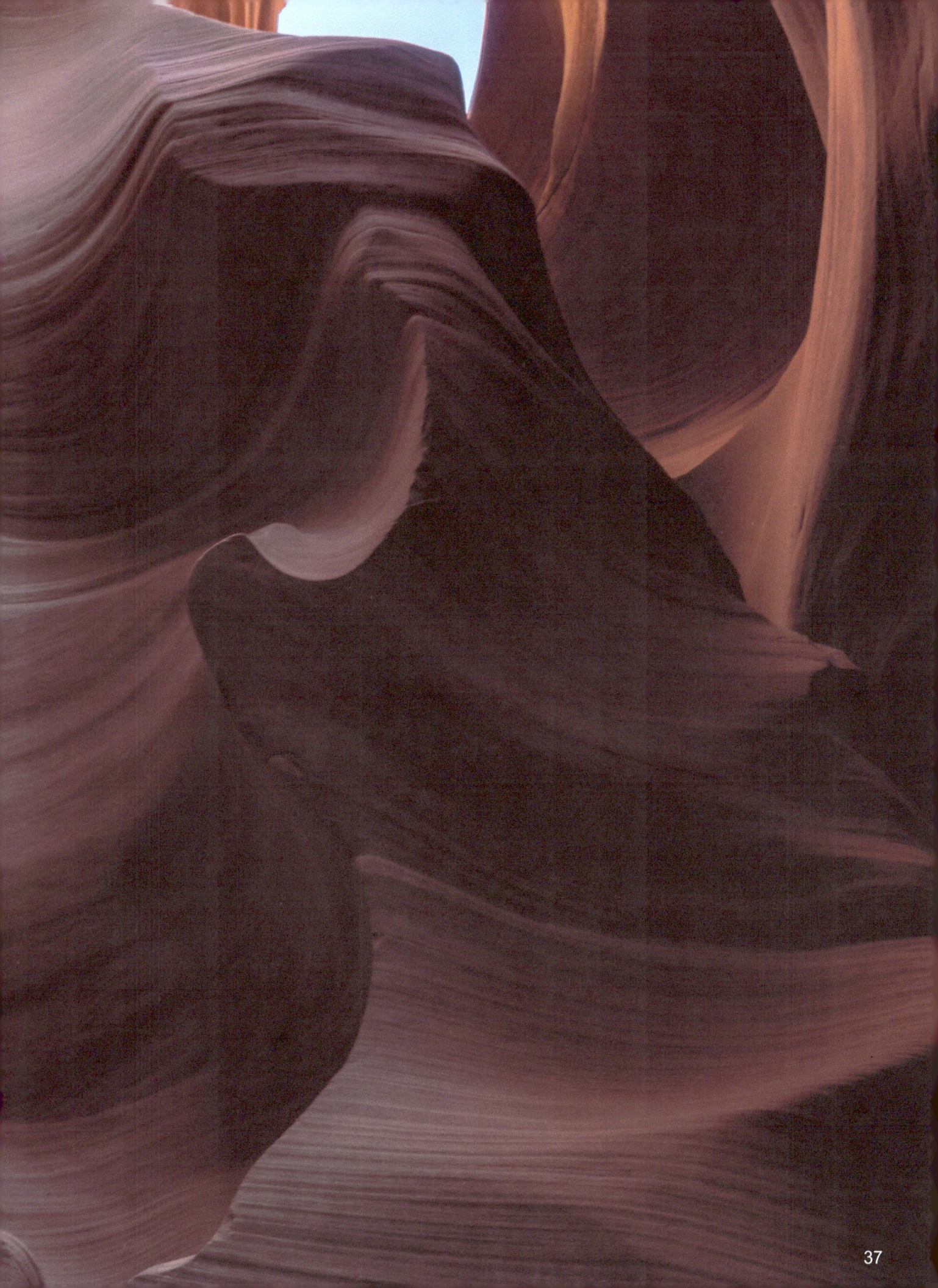

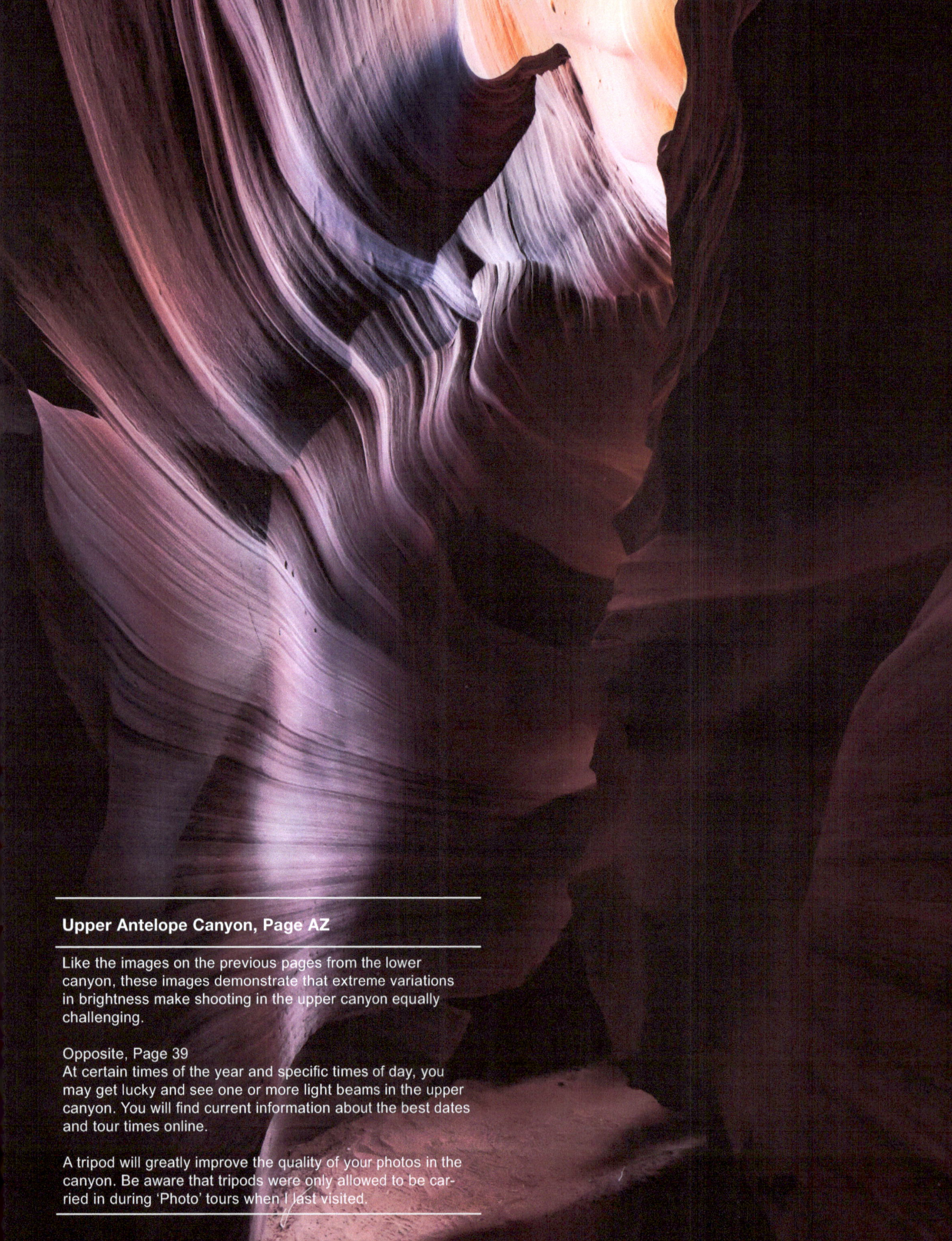

Upper Antelope Canyon, Page AZ

Like the images on the previous pages from the lower canyon, these images demonstrate that extreme variations in brightness make shooting in the upper canyon equally challenging.

Opposite, Page 39
At certain times of the year and specific times of day, you may get lucky and see one or more light beams in the upper canyon. You will find current information about the best dates and tour times online.

A tripod will greatly improve the quality of your photos in the canyon. Be aware that tripods were only allowed to be carried in during 'Photo' tours when I last visited.

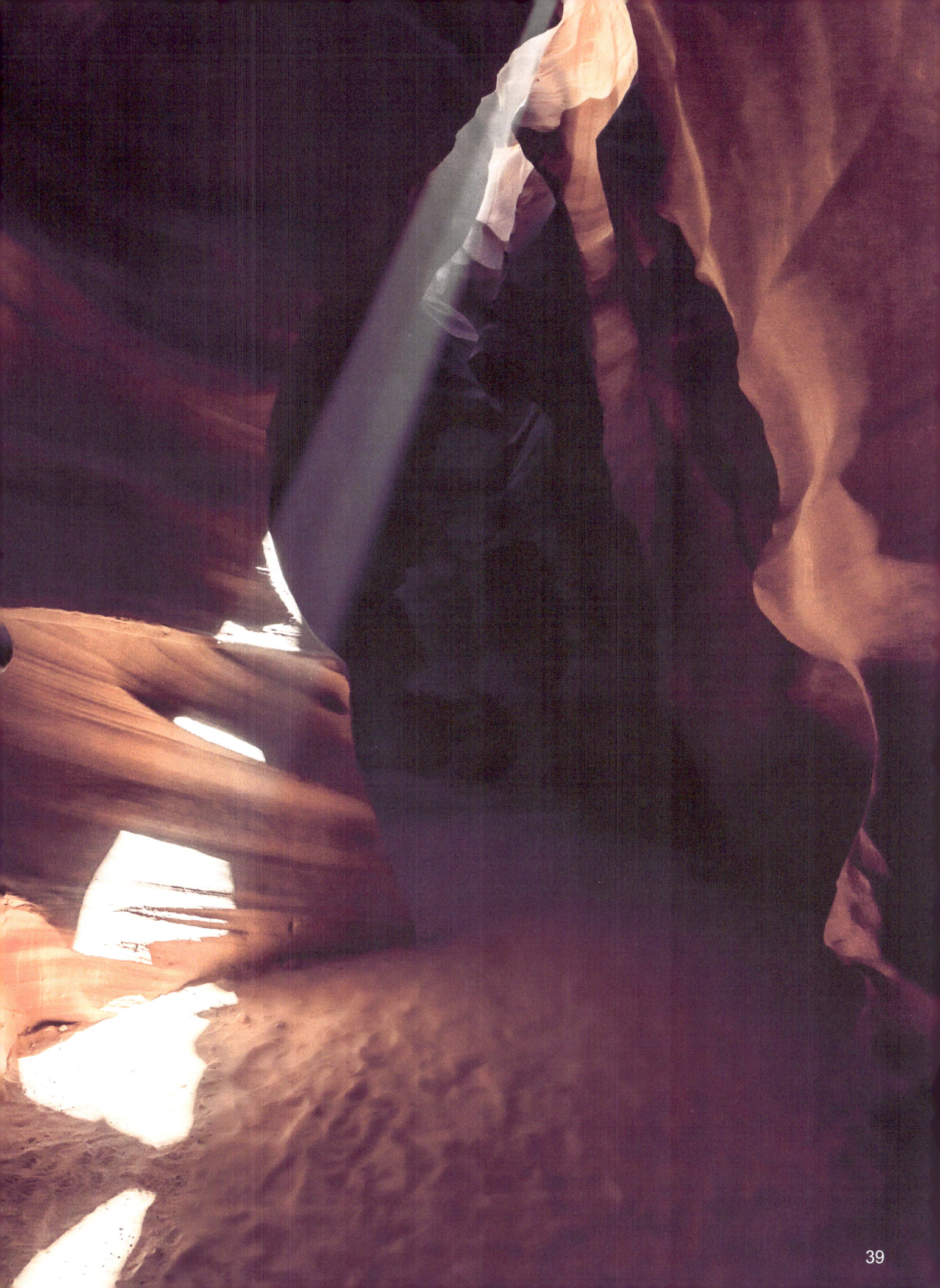

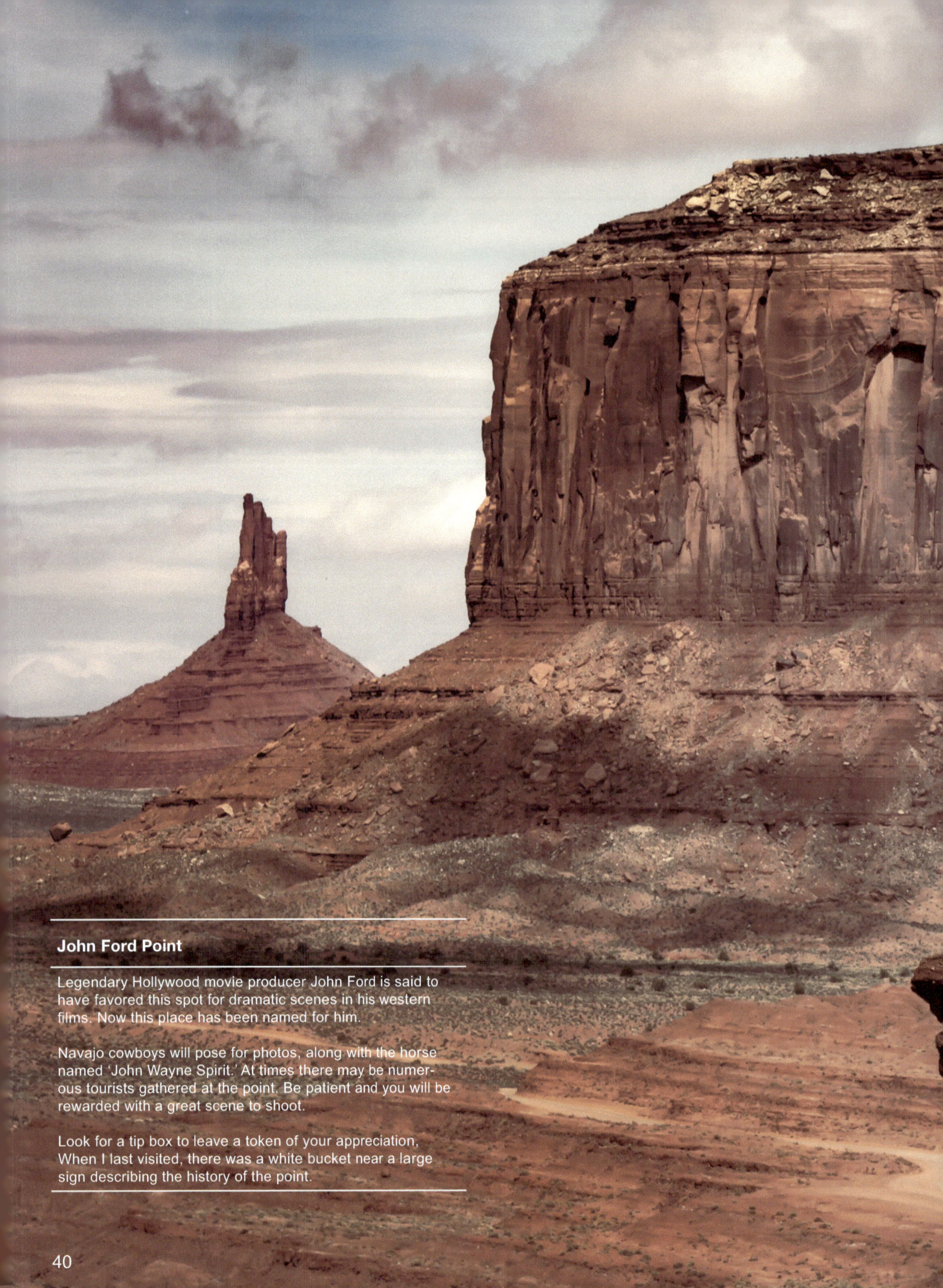

John Ford Point

Legendary Hollywood movie producer John Ford is said to have favored this spot for dramatic scenes in his western films. Now this place has been named for him.

Navajo cowboys will pose for photos, along with the horse named 'John Wayne Spirit.' At times there may be numerous tourists gathered at the point. Be patient and you will be rewarded with a great scene to shoot.

Look for a tip box to leave a token of your appreciation. When I last visited, there was a white bucket near a large sign describing the history of the point.

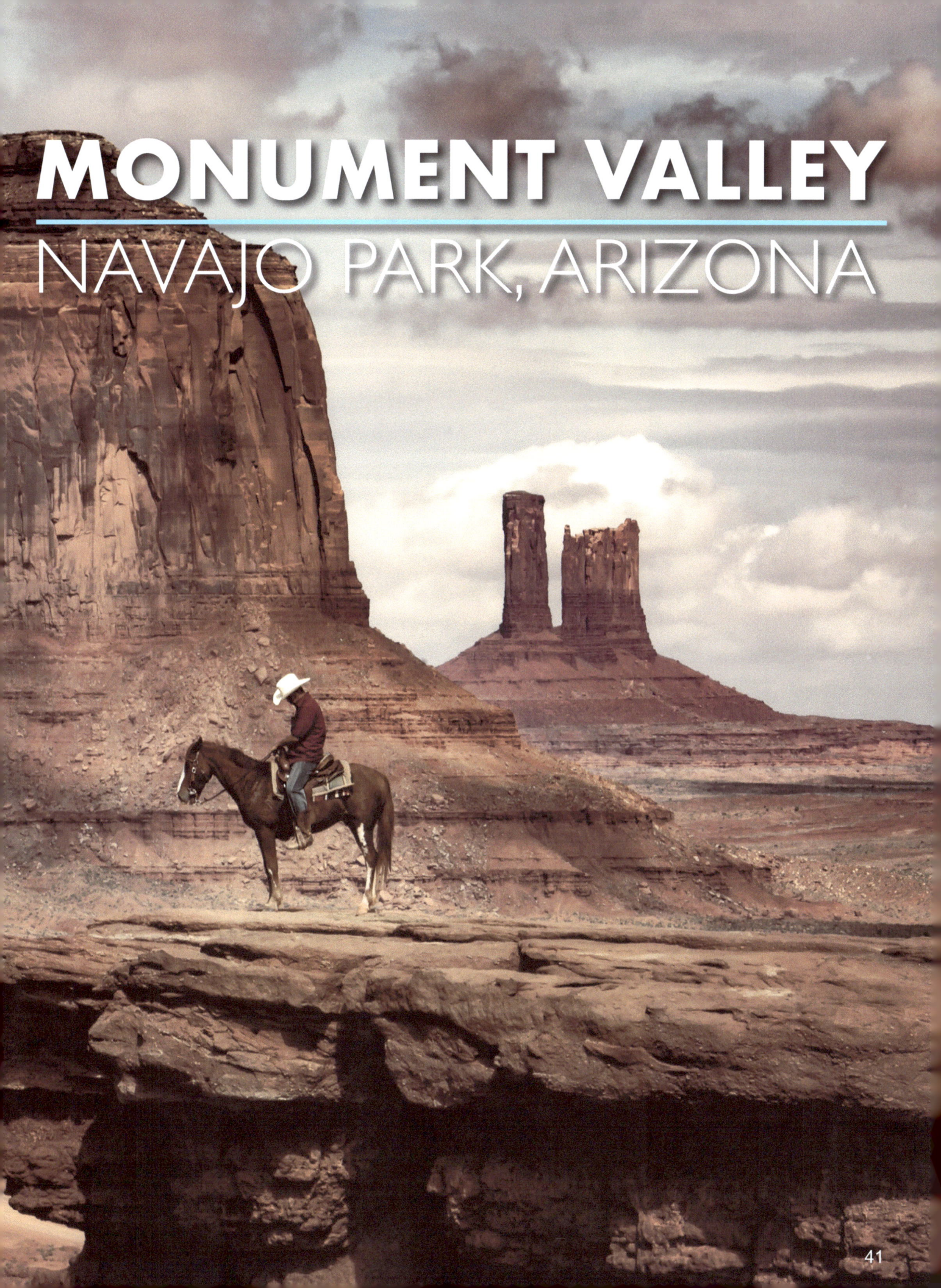

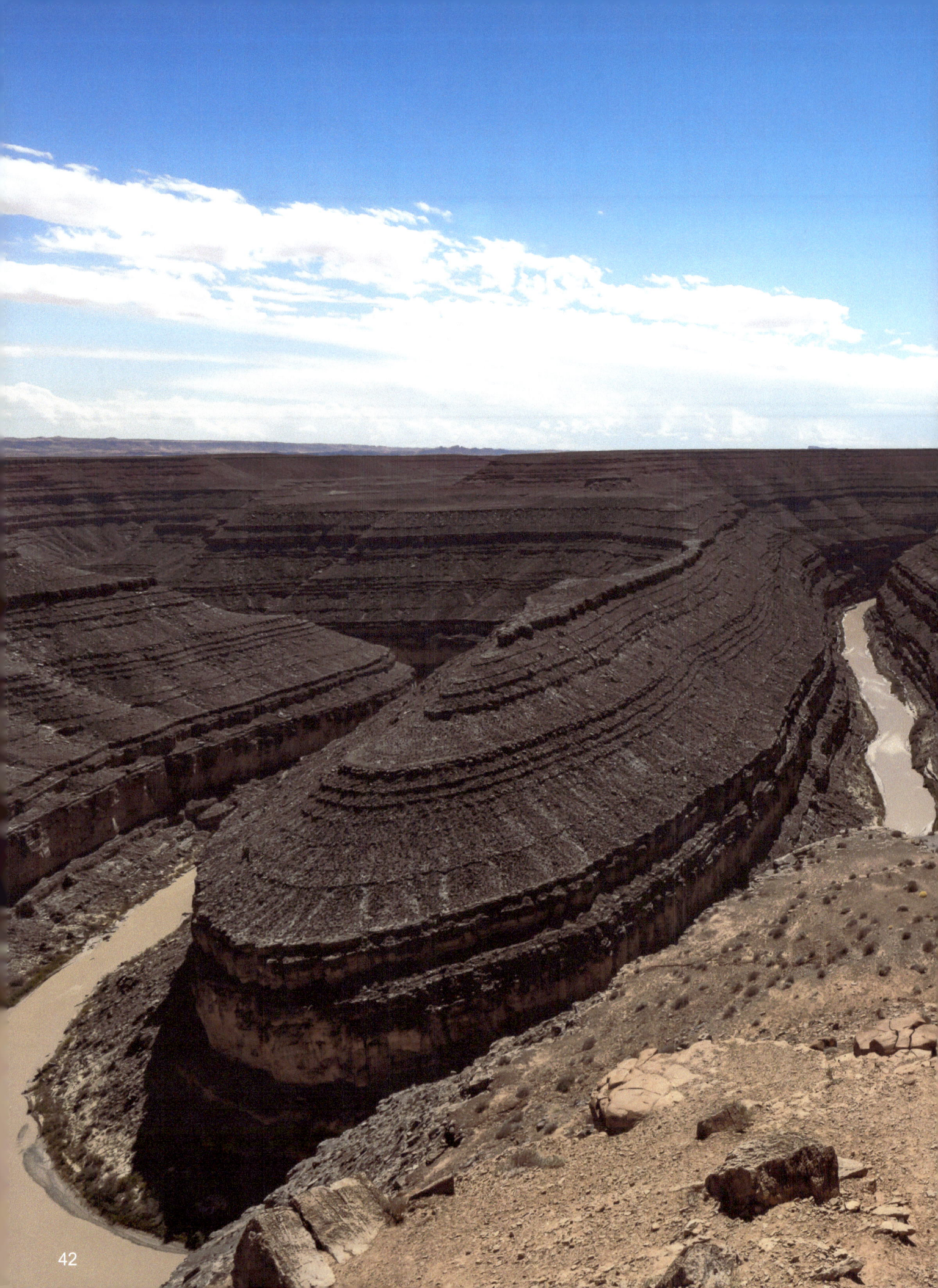

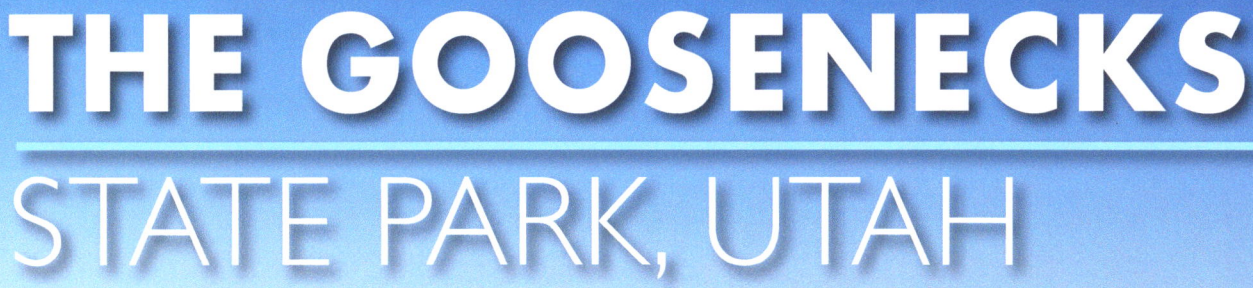

THE GOOSENECKS
STATE PARK, UTAH

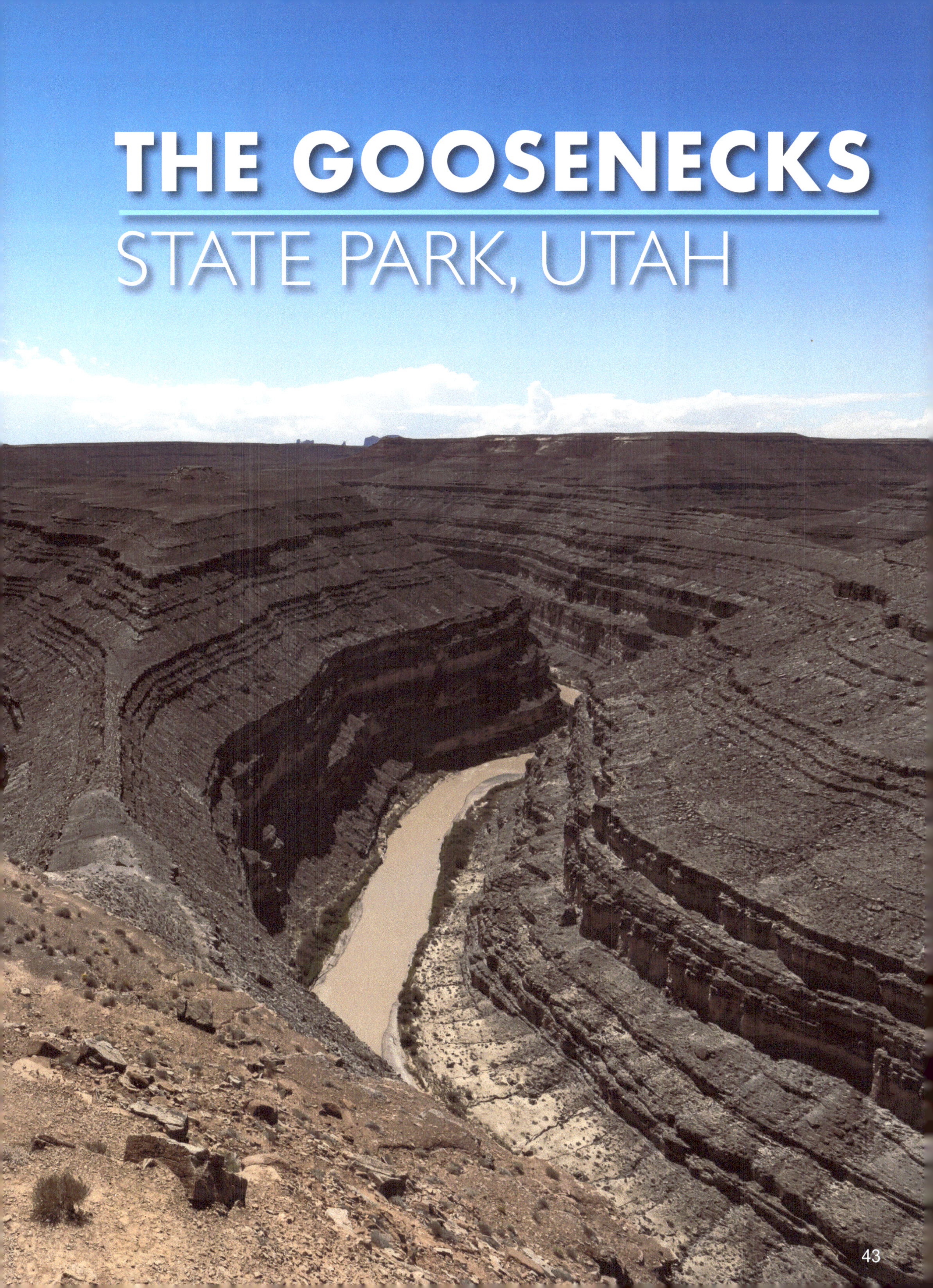

CAPITOL REEF
NATIONAL PARK, UTAH

Ancient Rock Art

Ancient artists discovered centuries ago how to cut through a thin patina layer on rock walls. Using this knowledge, they created many artistic and informational petroglyphs giving us a glimpse into their lives.

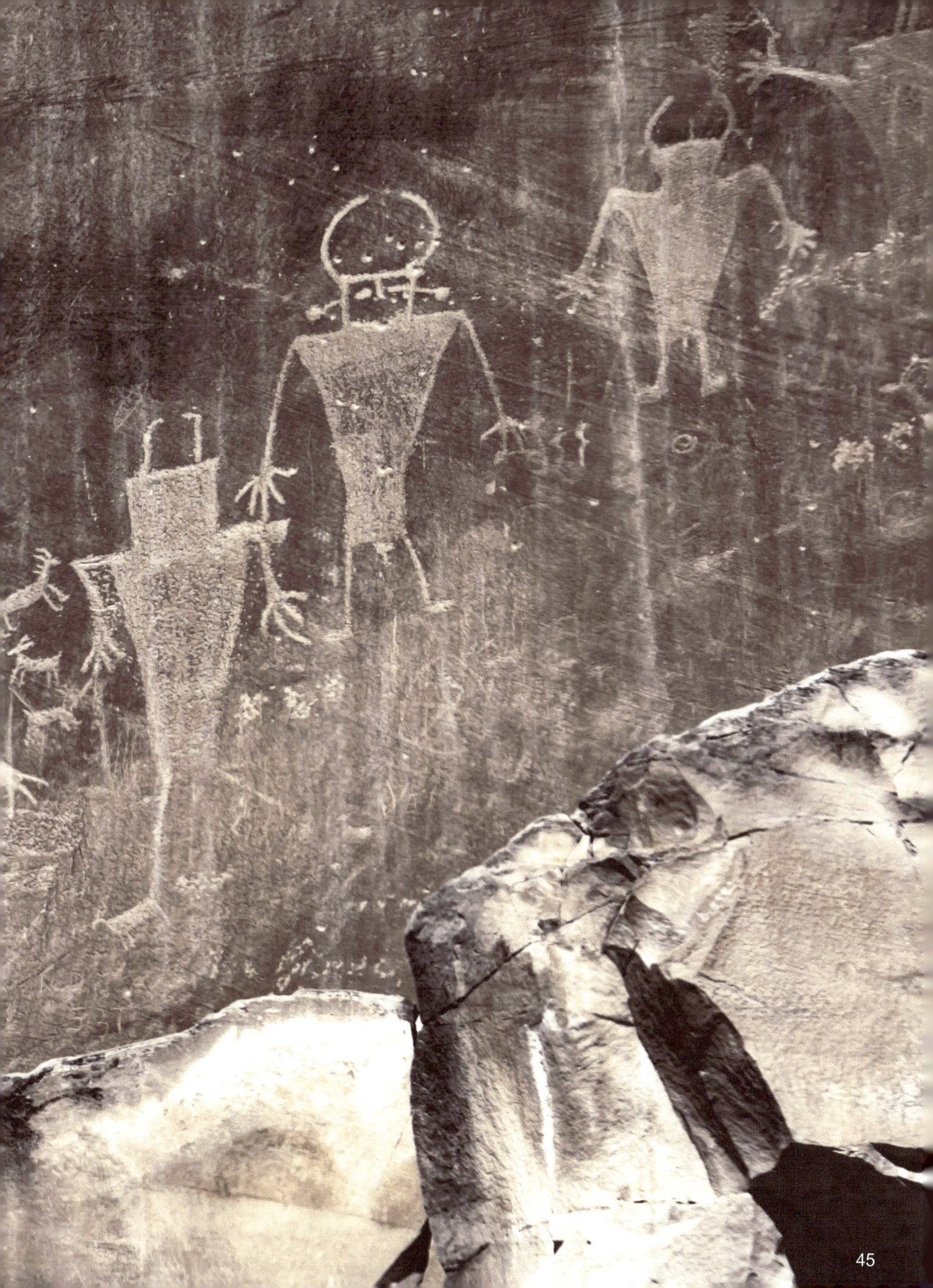

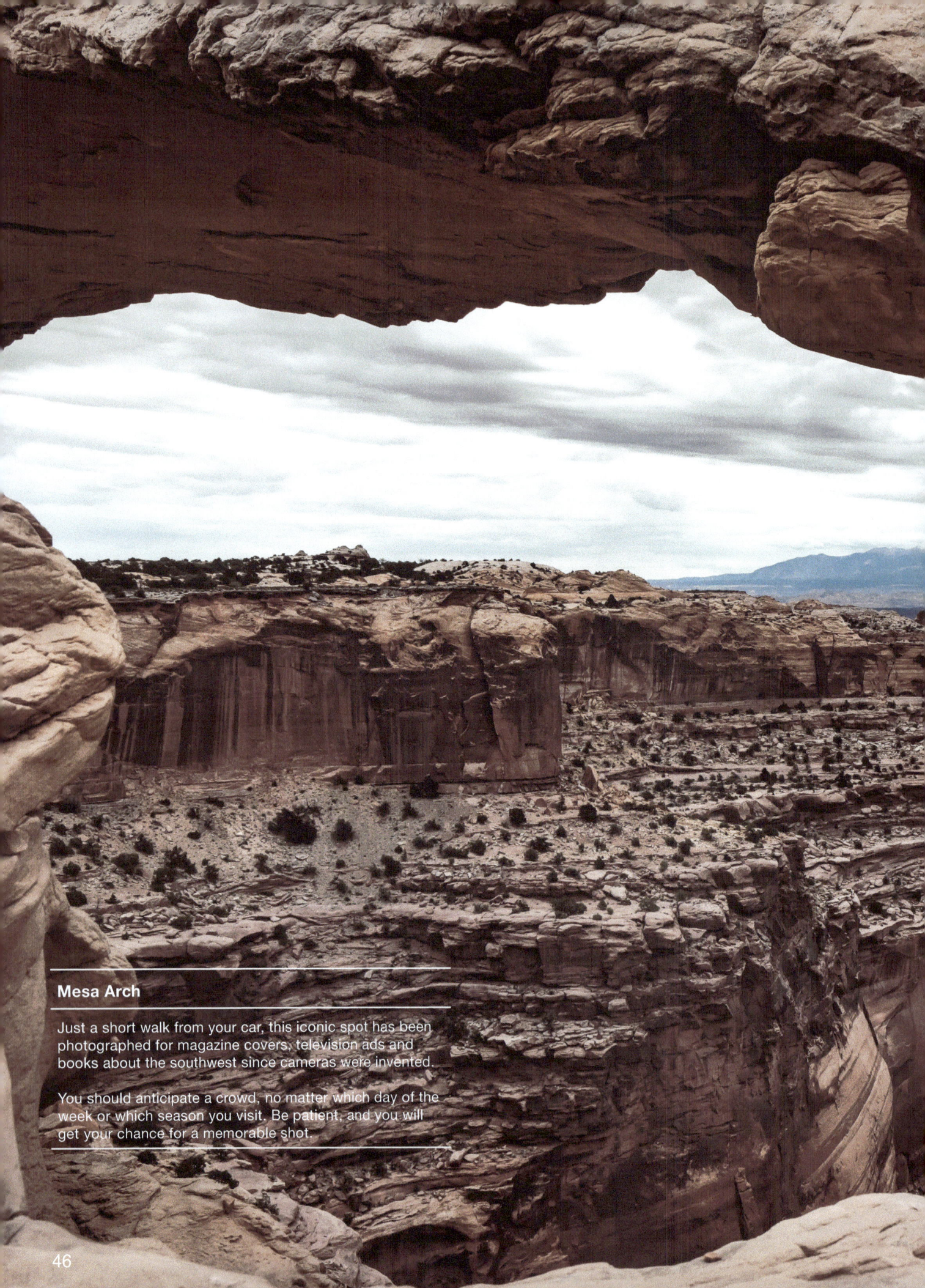

Mesa Arch

Just a short walk from your car, this iconic spot has been photographed for magazine covers, television ads and books about the southwest since cameras were invented.

You should anticipate a crowd, no matter which day of the week or which season you visit. Be patient, and you will get your chance for a memorable shot.

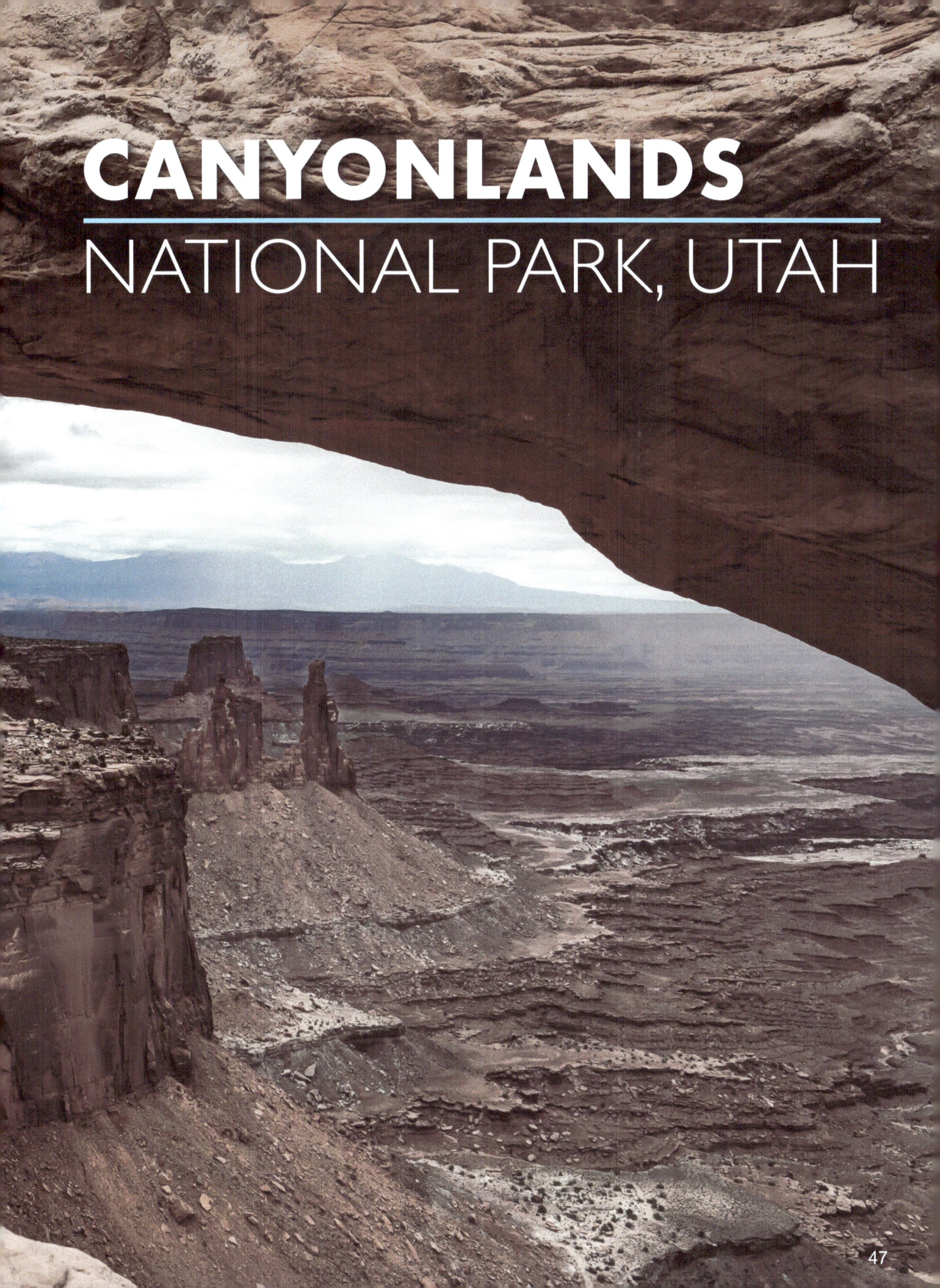

CANYONLANDS
NATIONAL PARK, UTAH

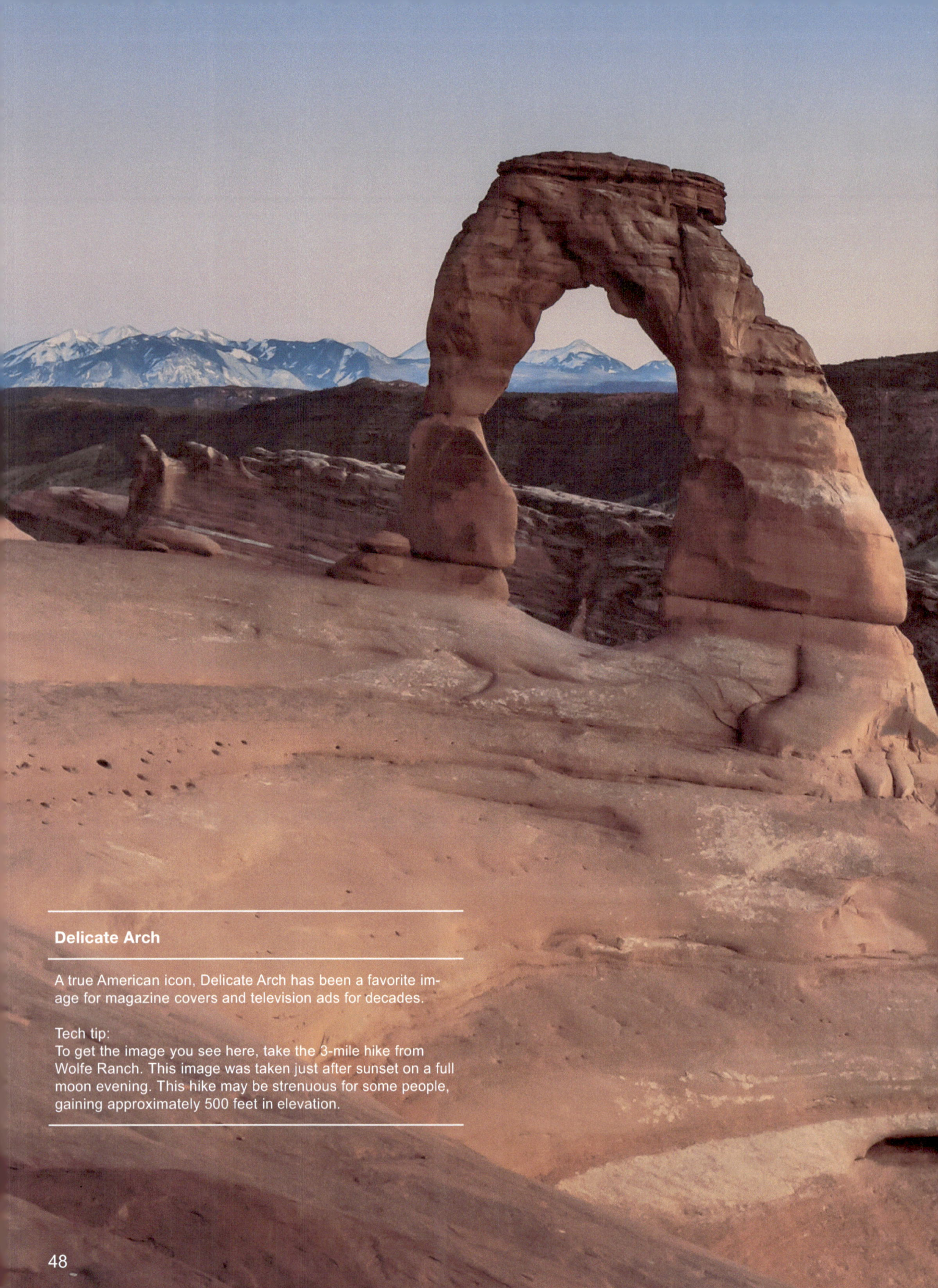

Delicate Arch

A true American icon, Delicate Arch has been a favorite image for magazine covers and television ads for decades.

Tech tip:
To get the image you see here, take the 3-mile hike from Wolfe Ranch. This image was taken just after sunset on a full moon evening. This hike may be strenuous for some people, gaining approximately 500 feet in elevation.

ARCHES
NATIONAL PARK, UTAH

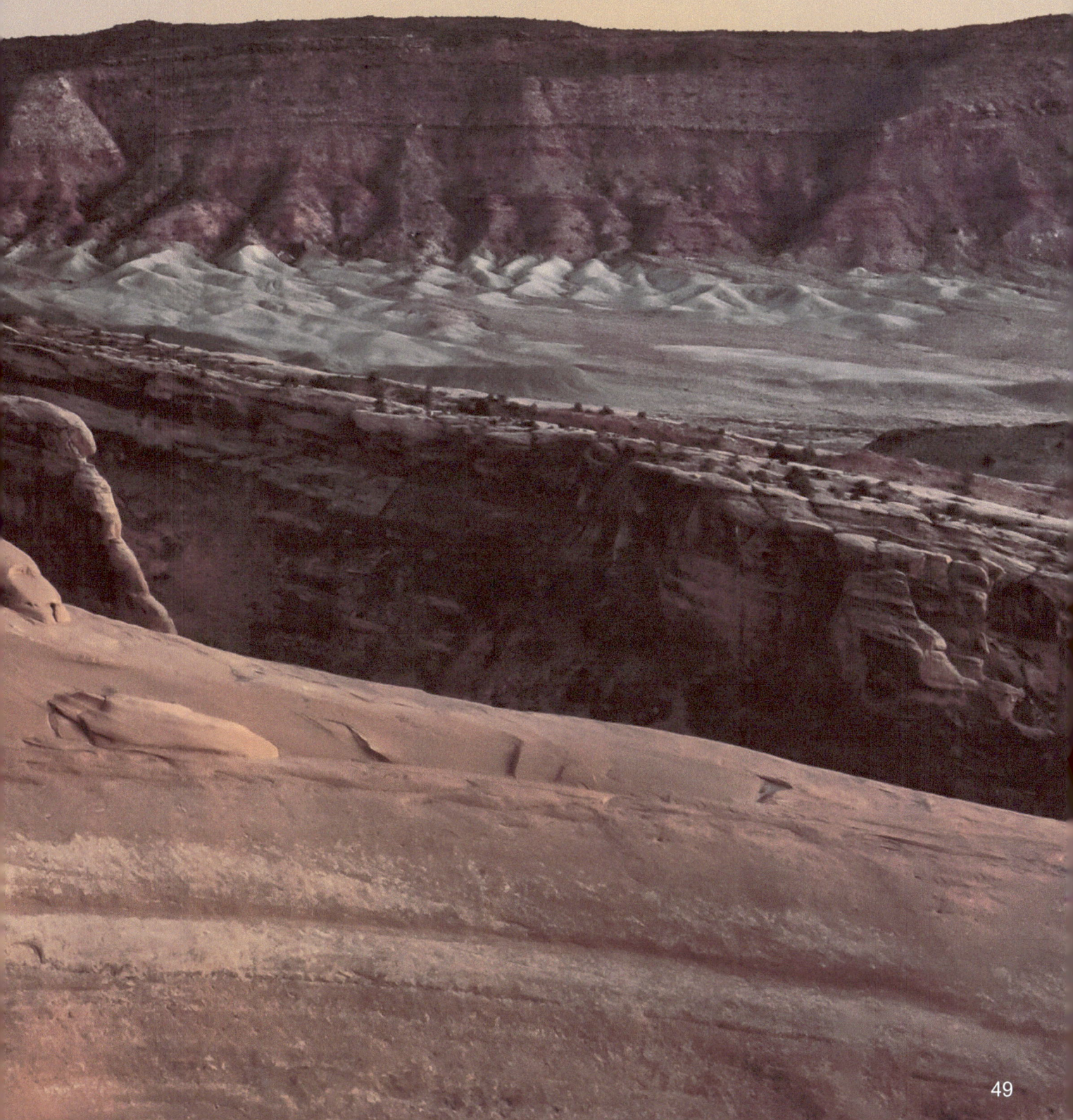

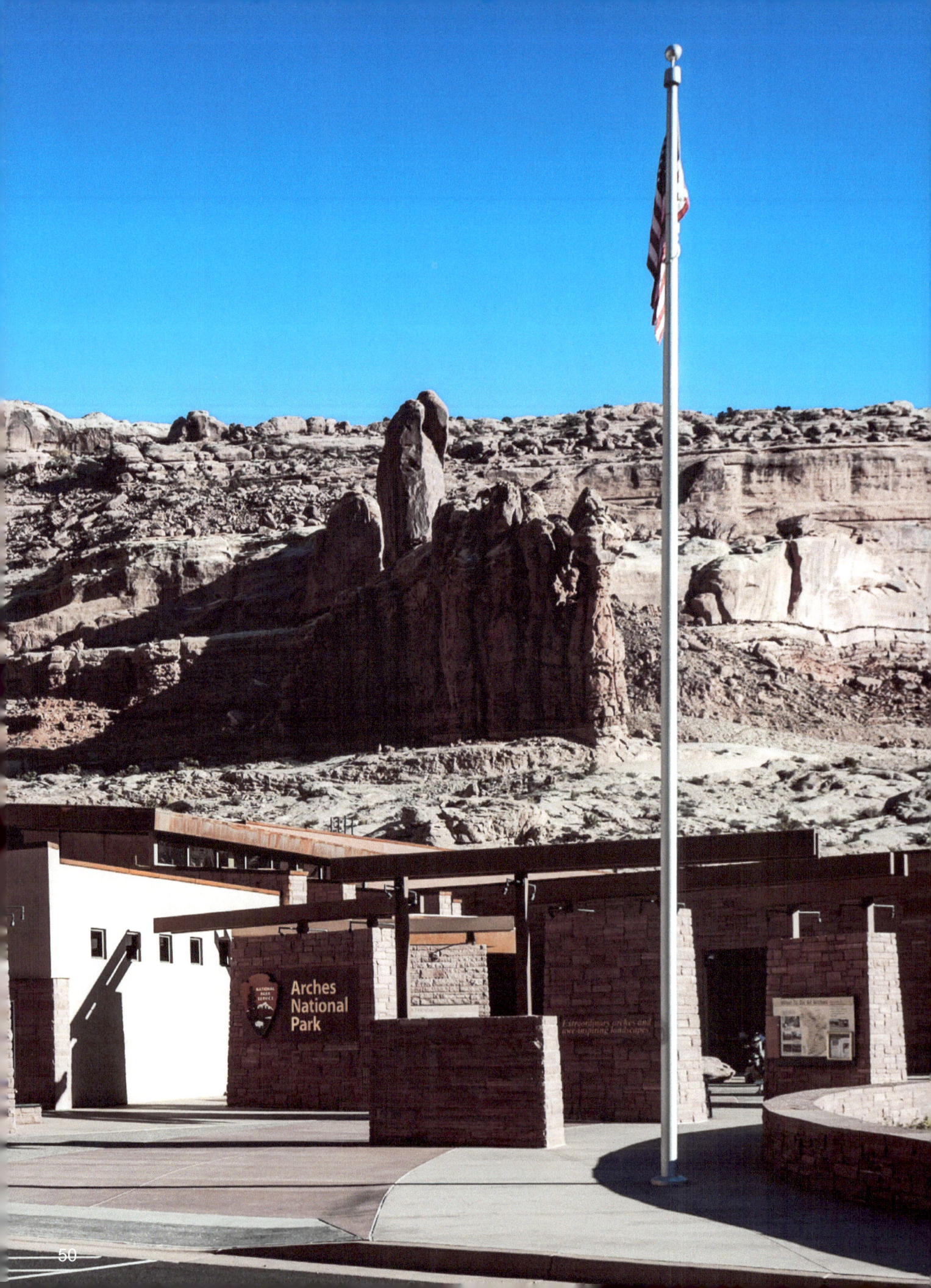

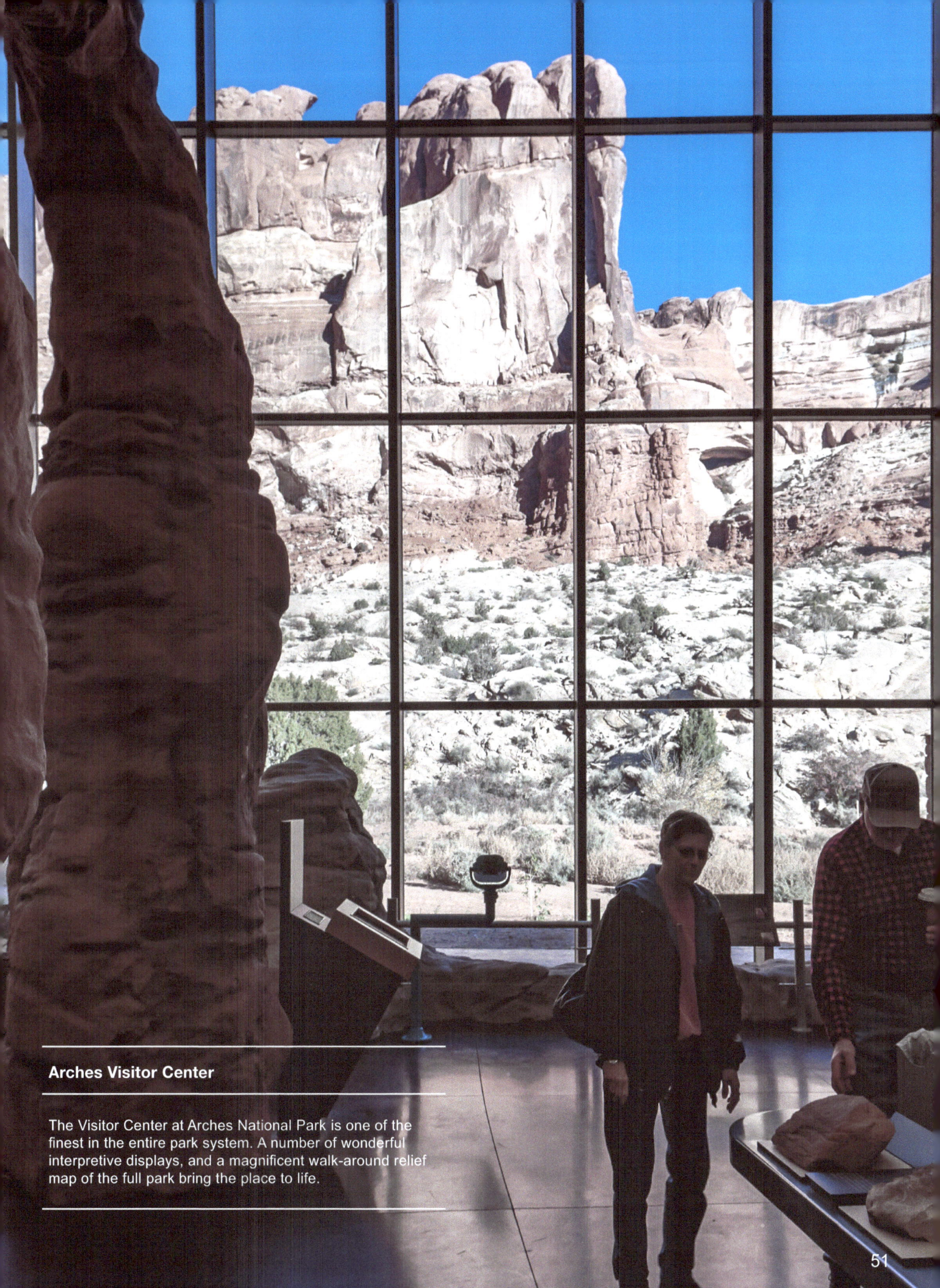

Arches Visitor Center

The Visitor Center at Arches National Park is one of the finest in the entire park system. A number of wonderful interpretive displays, and a magnificent walk-around relief map of the full park bring the place to life.

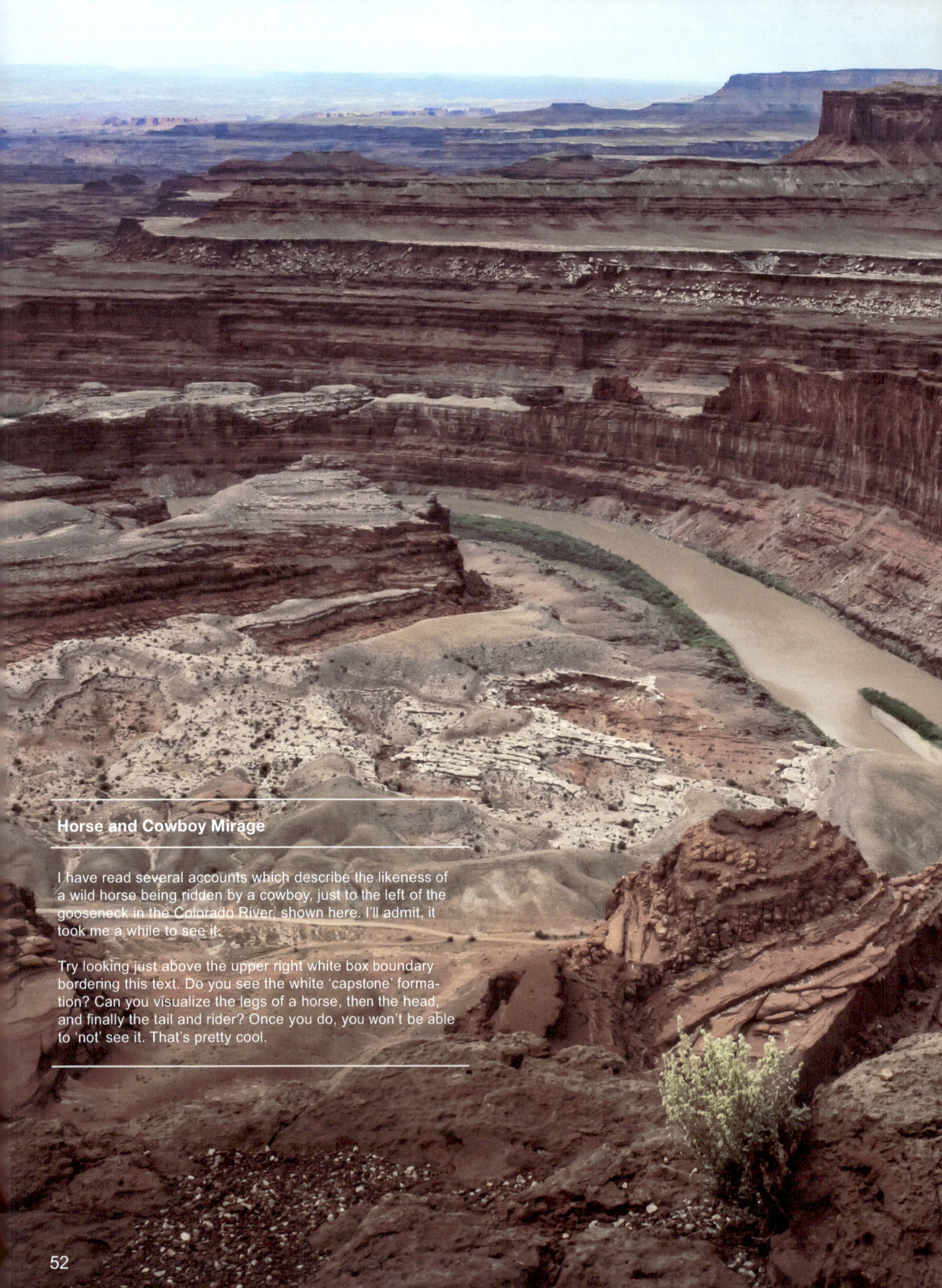

Horse and Cowboy Mirage

I have read several accounts which describe the likeness of a wild horse being ridden by a cowboy, just to the left of the gooseneck in the Colorado River, shown here. I'll admit, it took me a while to see it.

Try looking just above the upper right white box boundary bordering this text. Do you see the white 'capstone' formation? Can you visualize the legs of a horse, then the head, and finally the tail and rider? Once you do, you won't be able to 'not' see it. That's pretty cool.

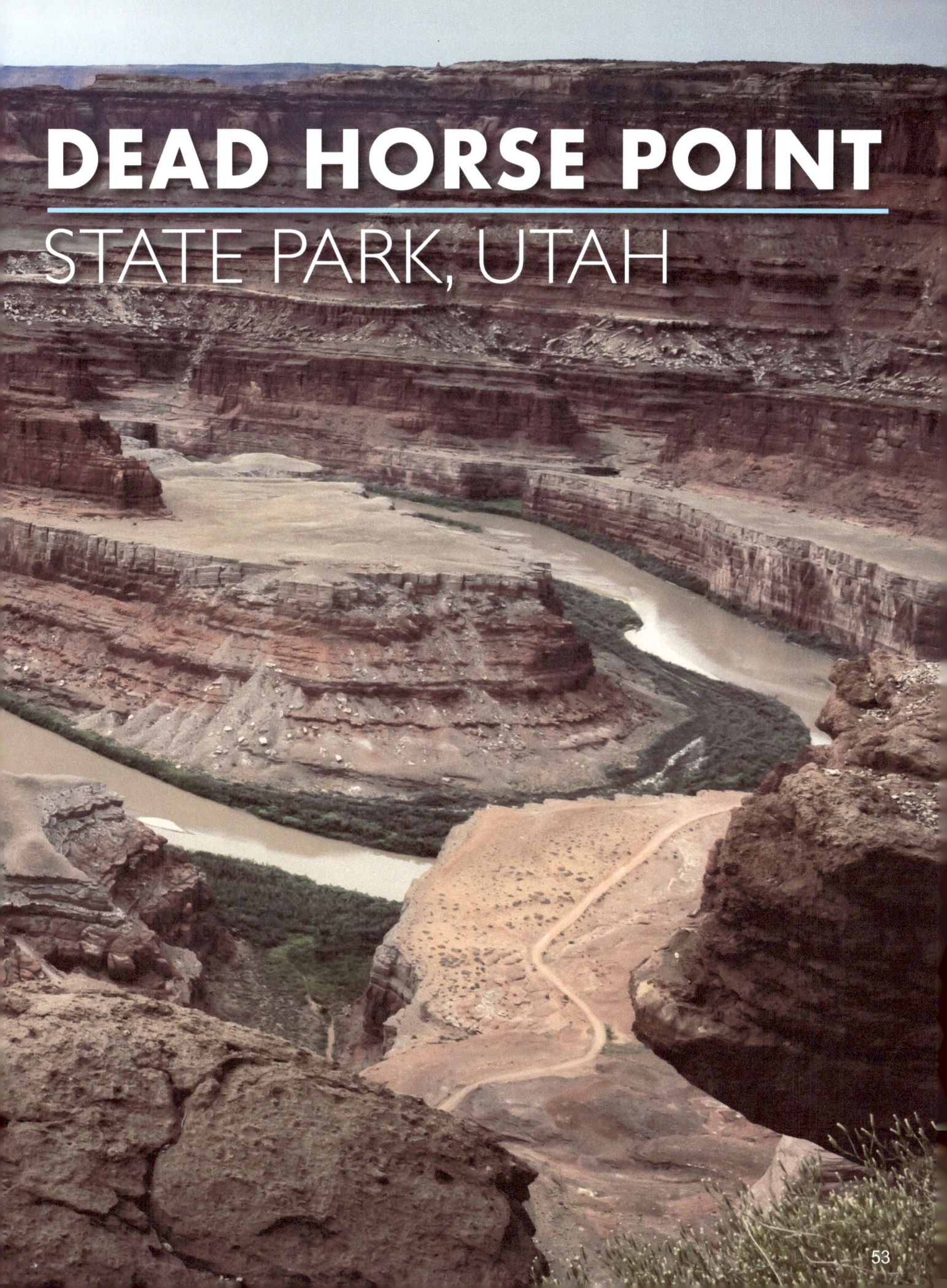

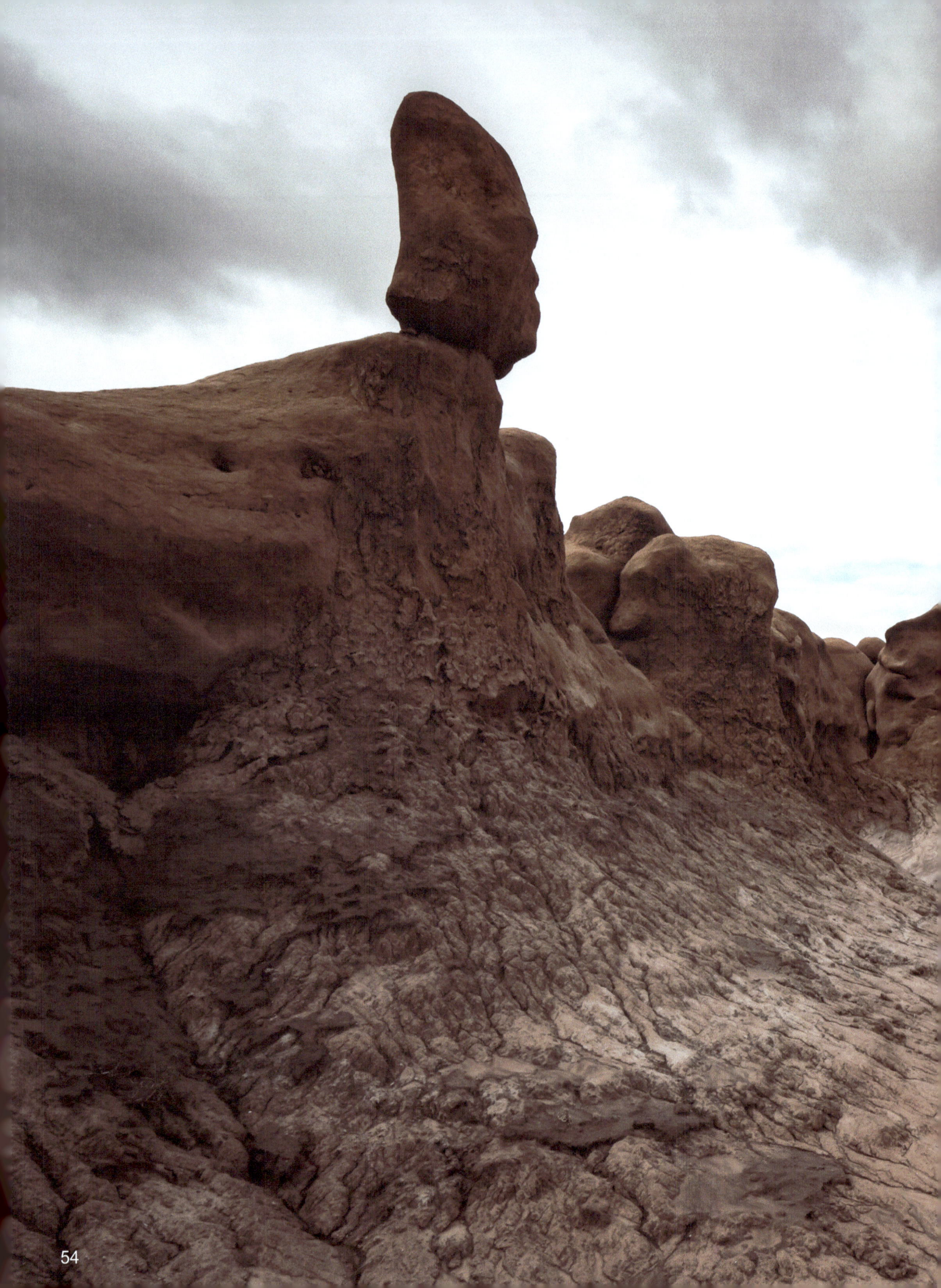

GOBLIN VALLEY
STATE PARK, UTAH

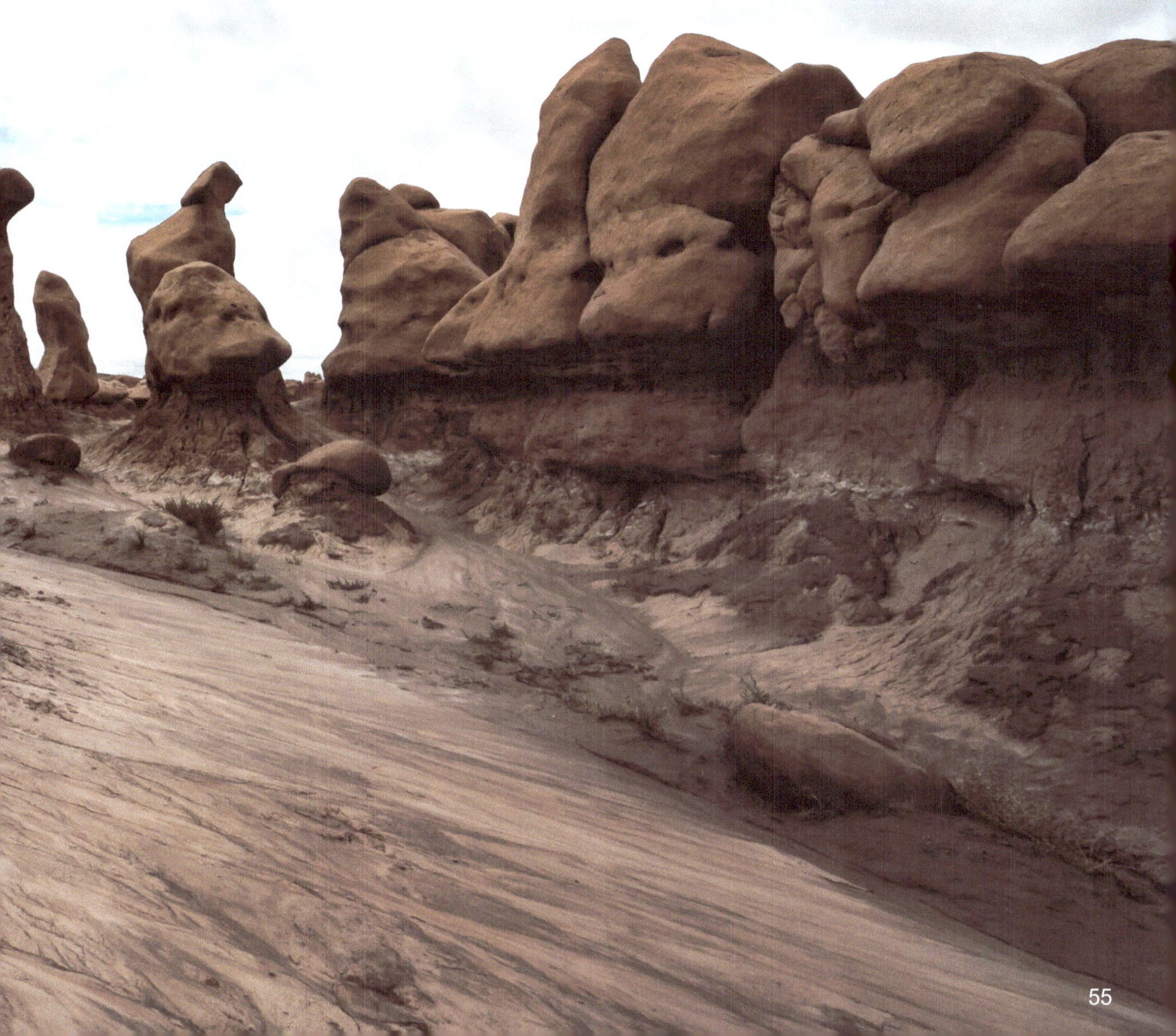

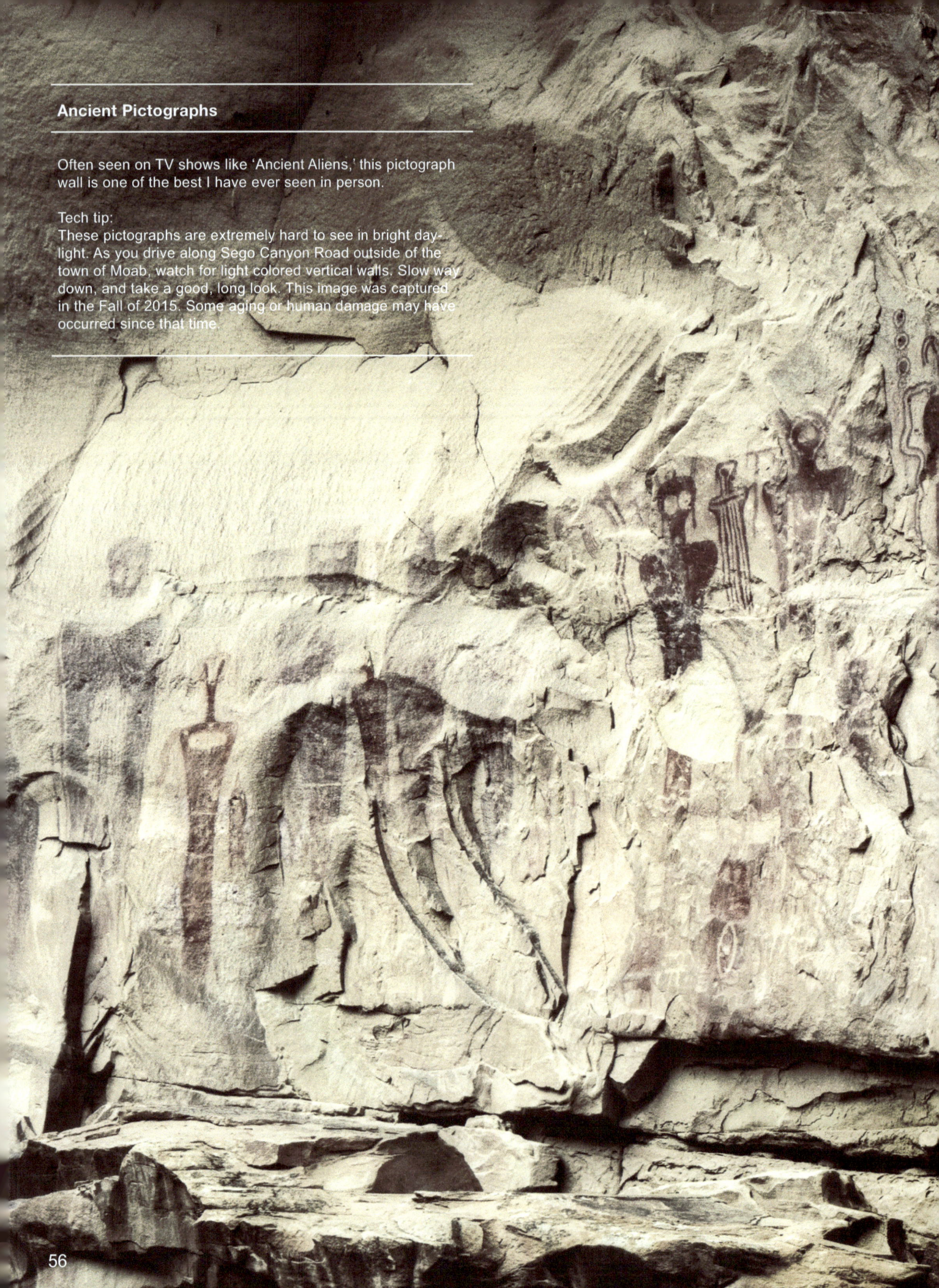

Ancient Pictographs

Often seen on TV shows like 'Ancient Aliens,' this pictograph wall is one of the best I have ever seen in person.

Tech tip:
These pictographs are extremely hard to see in bright daylight. As you drive along Sego Canyon Road outside of the town of Moab, watch for light colored vertical walls. Slow way down, and take a good, long look. This image was captured in the Fall of 2015. Some aging or human damage may have occurred since that time.

SEGO CANYON
HISTORIC SITE, UTAH

Beyond the Click

An Invitation

Thank you for purchasing and reading about my journey through a few of my favorite canyons of the southwest United States. I write and self-publish books of this type to share my work and (hopefully) to inspire a few readers to go out and experience these places, or places like them. If a few of you then decide to create art to document your memories, that will be wonderful! I invite you to think about what comes next for you.

Will you go out to experience places similar to those shown here? If so, will you use any of the planning or photo tips in this publication? I hope you will! In preparation for that, I have a few final, parting thoughts.

Artist, explorer, or both?

I invite you to consider how you want to experience your next exploration or adventure. There is no right or wrong way to experience a wild place, but there are very different experiences to be had. I, for example, consider myself an 'artist' whose brush is a camera, whose paint is a computer and software, and whose canvas is the print media upon which my visual art will be seen and, I hope, enjoyed by others.

I am also an 'explorer.' In fact, I was an explorer before I became an artist, as I traveled abroad for military service as a young man. That experience opened my mind to the realization that the world is a larger and even more wonderful collection of experiences than I had previously imagined. These experiences are available for everyone to enjoy. Tragically, too few of us actually have these experiences, for a variety of reasons.

My 'why,' the reason I explore and share

I explore and share my experiences so that other people might be inspired to do things and see places they may not otherwise do and see. A few of those people who are inspired to see and enjoy wild places may even become future stewards, which is a vision that inspires me to embark on even more adventures and share them with others, like you.

The medium I have chosen for sharing my message is the printed word, illustrated with works of art that I generate from a digital camera and illustrate on the printed page or, in some cases, on exquisite fine art paper or special metal print surfaces. With that said, it would be a disservice to you, the reader, if I stopped with that over-simplified description. In the interest of fairness and full disclosure, there is much more to the story of how these images are made.

Before and after the click

While it is true that this publication shares my experiences and images from several years visiting the places covered here, the truth is, there is much more to capturing great images of these parks than showing up there with a camera.

Most of my photo trips are quite different than a typical traveler would undertake. For example, in recent years, I have travelled with a small group by truck instead of aircraft. This enables us take an extensive set of equipment with us. I have had the advantage of a collection of lenses, filters, tripods, batteries, and incidental tools required to make these images possible.

To the Artist: The click is only the beginning

Communication is the artist's objective. My objective is to share the feeling I had when I stood at a place. I never have forgotten the sensory experience of a place that moved me - the height of the mountains, the smell of the pines, the sound of the wind in the trees or the roar of a nearby river.

For my fellow photographers desiring to make a stronger connection with your audience, in my experience communication through imagery is not a function of technical perfection. Sharpness, saturation and contrast are not as important as your composition and imact of the scene. I like to visit some places over and over, and I try to get images that evoke different emotional reactions, like clear skies with white puffy clouds as well as angry, stormy skies, or even the lucky rainbow just as a shower passes and the sun returns. Each of these images will evoke different reactions in the viewer.

Art is about emotion

All images shown in this publication have been processed using software that enables me to 'shape' the image in such a way that it helps me recall how I felt when I captured it. I often think back to a time when I was first learning digital photography. I would go someplace hoping to get stunning images like those I saw online or in photo books, but I failed every time, because I had not yet become an artist.

Before I share images in print, I process them in a way that will evoke emotion in my reader. My tips are intended to be helpful, but the truth is, most people will not have invested the time and expense that I have. Just know that your images are your own - you were there!

Forever a student

Anyone willing to take the artist's journey can match or exceed the image 'quality' seen in this or any other publication. Yes, you can! Let me share a few tips to get you started on your journey:

Be forever a student

> Study everything about your subjects
> Ask questions
> Listen to what others have to say
> Share
> Experiment

Learn what "style" is, and develop yours

Know "why" you make art and commit to it

Be disciplined

Question everything you do

Make good art, and only good art

Closing thoughts

I have shared this story in the hope that you will be inspired get outside and have your own experiences. Your experience will be yours to remember. Some of you may want to share your experiences, and I hope I have given that group some ideas and inspiration to inspire others.

Larry Rogers

About the Author

Larry Rogers has been photographing national parks and wildlife for more than 40 years. Formally educated in electrical engineering and computer science, Larry was given his first camera around age 8 and cannot recall a time when he did not have a camera.

Following graduation from college, he served as an Air Defense Officer in the US Army, a US government civilian employee and small business owner. But, throughout, his passion for wildlife, wild places, and the environment fueled his love of photography and the arts.

With a burning passion to constantly learn and develop his art to a high level, Larry is now extending his art to new perspectives, flying a drone and publishing books which he hopes will inspire the next generation of conservation and nature photographers.

He currently lives in southwest Ohio, in the United States. He is the father of two sons, and grandfather to two granddaughters.

Larry welcomes readers to follow and/or contact him via social media, email or comments on his website.

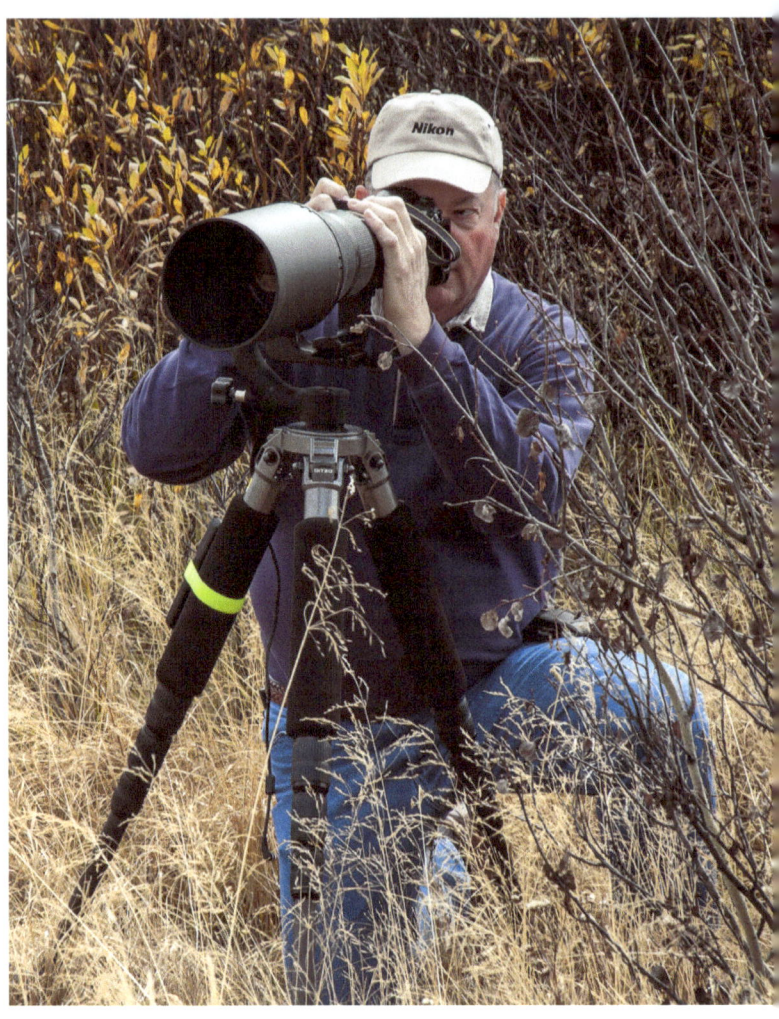

Contact

Instagram: larryrogersartandmotion
LinkedIn: linkedin.com/in/the-conservancy-project
email: inquire@larryrogers.us
Twitter: @larryrogers
Website: larryrogersphotography.us

Follow us on Instagram for up-to-date information on new products and current projects.

More from Larry Rogers

eBooks available in the iBooks Store
Getting the Shot: Yellowstone
Getting the Shot: Death Valley

eBooks available on Amazon
Yellowstone: Enigma in Fire & Water

Art prints are available at larryrogersphotography.us
Yellowstone Landscapes
Yellowstone Wildlife
Grand Teton National Park
and many more galleries

Be safe in your travels, and remember, "Take only photographs, and leave only footprints!"

www.ingramcontent.com/pod-product-compliance
Lightning Source LLC
Chambersburg PA
CBHW051211220526
45473CB00003B/985